R...ICISM

...BASICS

From the basic ideas and terms, to its structures and practices, this book offers a plain-speaking introduction to Roman Catholicism. It covers:

- Roman Catholic beliefs and traditions;
- practices and devotional life – rituals, prayer, mass;
- the Church structures and authorities – from Vatican to parish church;
- the Church hierarchies and people – from bishops to the laity;
- the role of the Church in society.

With glossary, further reading sections and an appendix on the History of the Papacy, this is the perfect guide for anyone wanting to understand more about Roman Catholicism.

Michael Walsh has retired recently as Librarian of Heythrop College, University of London. He now edits the *Heythrop Journal*. A former Jesuit, he has written on many aspects of the history of Christianity, and especially on the contemporary Church.

You may also be interested in the following Routledge Student Reference titles:

RELIGION: THE BASICS
Malory Nye

FIFTY KEY CHRISTIAN THINKERS
Peter McEnhill and George Newlands

FIFTY KEY JEWISH THINKERS
Dan Cohn-Sherbok

THE ROUTLEDGE DICTIONARY OF JUDAISM
Jacob Neusner and Alan J. Avery-Peck

GURDJIEFF: THE KEY CONCEPTS
Sophia Wellbeloved

EASTERN PHILOSOPHY: KEY READINGS
Oliver Leaman

KEY CONCEPTS IN EASTERN PHILOSOPHY
Oliver Leaman

FIFTY EASTERN THINKERS
Diané Collinson, Kathryn Plant and Robert Wilkinson

WHO'S WHO IN CHRISTIANITY
Lavinia Cohn-Sherbok

WHO'S WHO IN JEWISH HISTORY
Joan Comay; new edition revised by Lavinia Cohn-Sherbok

WHO'S WHO IN THE NEW TESTAMENT
Ronald Brownrigg

WHO'S WHO IN THE OLD TESTAMENT
Joan Comay

ROMAN CATHOLICISM
THE BASICS

michael walsh

Routledge
Taylor & Francis Group

LONDON AND NEW YORK

First published 2005 by Routledge
2 Park Square, Milton Park, Abingdon, Oxon OX14 4RN

Simultaneously published in the USA and Canada
by Taylor & Francis Inc.
270 Madison Ave., New York, NY 10016

Routledge is an imprint of the Taylor & Francis Group

© 2005 Michael Walsh

Typeset in Aldus Roman and Scala Sans by Taylor & Francis Books
Printed and bound in Great Britain by MPG Books Ltd, Bodmin, Cornwall

British Library Cataloguing in Publication Data
A catalogue record for this book is available from the British Library

Library of Congress Cataloging-in-Publication Data
Walsh, Michael J., 1937–
   Roman Catholicism: The Basics / Michael Walsh.
      p. cm.
Includes bibliographical references (p.) and index
ISBN 0-415-26381-6 (pbk.) – ISBN 0-415-26380-8 (hardback)
   1. Catholic Church–Doctrines. I. Title
      BX1751.3.W35 2005
      282–dc22

ISBN 0–415–26380–8 (hbk)
ISBN 0–415–26381–6 (pbk)

CONTENTS

ILLUSTRATIONS

BOXES

INTRODUCTION

WHAT DO CATHOLICS BELIEVE?

A book with the title *Roman Catholicism: The Basics* might quite properly be expected to begin with a chapter on what Catholics believe. And in a sense it is an easy question to answer. What Catholics believe is summed up in a series of short, formal statements called 'creeds' (from the Latin *credere* meaning 'to believe'). There are a number of these creeds, mainly dating from the earliest centuries of Christianity when they were used as statements of faith for people being initiated into the religion. The best-known creed, the Nicene creed, comes from the fourth century and takes its name from a gathering of bishops of the Church which took place in AD 325 at Nicaea, the modern Iznik in Turkey. The formulation that is now in use (see box) is a development of the AD 325 version, and is accepted by most, if not all, Christian Churches – though one important group object to the phrase 'and from the Son', not because they do not believe it so much as because it was added to the Nicene creed much later.

While it is true that this is the statement of faith which Catholics and others recite when they go to church on Sundays, there are a great many problems with it as a guide to Christianity. First of all, it is very difficult to understand. A good deal of it reflects rather arcane debates in the fourth century which very few people nowadays know anything at all about. Second, it certainly does not cover everything that Catholics or other Christians believe – as we shall see in the rest of this book. And third, because most Christians accept it, it does not really serve to distinguish Roman Catholics from other Christian groups.

None the less it states some things about Christianity which anyone coming to the study of Christianity needs to know about the faith before they begin more detailed examination of Roman Catholicism.

THE NICENE CREED

We believe in one god, the Father, the Almighty, maker of heaven and earth, of all that is, seen and unseen.

We believe in one Lord, Jesus Christ, the only Son of God, eternally begotten of the Father, God from God, Light from Light, true God from true God, begotten, not made, of one being with the Father.

Through him all things were made.

For us and for our salvation he came down from heaven: by the power of the Holy Spirit he became incarnate from the Virgin Mary and was made man.

For our sake he was crucified under Pontius Pilate; he suffered death and was buried.

On the third day he rose again in accordance with the Scriptures; he ascended into heaven and is seated at the right hand of the Father.

He will come again in glory to judge the living and the dead, and his kingdom will have no end.

We believe in the Holy Spirit, the Lord, the giver of life, who proceeds from the Father and the Son.

With the Father and the Son he is worshipped and glorified.

He has spoken through the prophets.

We believe in one holy, catholic and apostolic Church.

We acknowledge one baptism for the forgiveness of sins.

We look for the resurrection of the dead and the life of the world to come.

Amen.

THE TRINITY

First of all, then, almost all Christians believe not only in the existence of God, but in the existence of a Trinitarian God. That is to say, they believe that, although there is only one God, he or she (God must be above, or transcend, gender differences) exists in three 'persons', the Father, the Son, and the Holy Spirit. In other words, God is, as it were, a community. It is important to understand that the three persons *do not* constitute three gods. Christians do not think, as the ancient Greeks seemed to, that there is a family of gods, who squabble among themselves and who are really only different from us by being much more powerful.

I am not going to try to explain this three-in-oneness of God. It is not something that human beings would ever think up for themselves. It comes from God revealing him/herself in the sacred writings which Christians call 'the Scriptures' ('Scripture' means 'writing' in Latin). Of course, once we know about the three-in-oneness by way of the Scriptures, we can reflect on it and come up with theories about it. But to do so here would lead us into some extremely difficult questions of philosophy and theology, which have no place in this book – though I will talk a little about the role of philosophy and theology themselves later on in this Introduction.

The second of the three 'persons' is referred to as the Son, of whom it says in the Creed that he 'was made man'.

THE INCARNATION

The technical expression for being 'made man' is incarnation, which again is a term which comes from the Latin, this time from *caro* meaning 'flesh'. Christians believe that the second person of the Trinity became man, and was born of Mary, as the creed says. God the Son became a human being, and lived on earth as Jesus Christ ('Christ' is a title rather than a name, and means 'anointed'). So Jesus was – is – God. In Jesus the nature of God and the nature of a human being were united in one person. This uniting of the two natures in the one person of Jesus is known technically as the 'hypostatic union', from the Greek 'hypostasis' meaning, literally, 'substance'.

Again, this is a very difficult idea, and not one anyone would believe had it not been revealed in the life of Jesus, but, as with the

Trinity, there are theological and philosophical ways of thinking about the fact, once it is known through revelation. But in a sense the central question for Christians is why did Jesus become a human being?

THE REDEMPTION

It is central to Christian belief that God created the universe and all that is in it ('maker of heaven and earth, of all that is, seen and unseen'). That God is creator does not necessarily mean that the universe had a beginning, because God is outside time. Some Christians believe in the literal truth of the writings which make up the Christian scriptures, and in one of those writing, called the Book of Genesis, God is presented as creating the universe in six days. Catholics, while they are not bound to so literal an understanding of the creation story in Genesis, accept that God is a creator God, and that human beings, created by God, became alienated from him in the 'Fall' when, again as recounted in Genesis, the first two people, named in Genesis as Adam and Eve, offended against God. The purpose of God's becoming a man was to overcome that alienation. It was to bring humankind back to God that Jesus was incarnated. He brought humanity back to God through his life, his death and his resurrection from the dead. Winning human beings back to God is called redemption.

But redemption from what? Again as the creed makes clear, Christians believe that there is life after death. The redemption means that human beings need not be separated from God but, in the next life, can be united with him/her. So redemption means being saved from eternal alienation from God, in other words being saved from a state known as being in hell. However, human beings have to be judged worthy of that union with God – hence in the creed 'He will come again in glory to judge the living and the dead'.

DOGMA

These, then, are some of the most basic statements about the Christian faith. Roman Catholics call them 'dogmas' or dogmatic statements. Dogmatic statements are statements which Catholics are obliged to accept as true because they are an essential part of their faith. However, you don't 'have faith' in dogmas themselves: they are expressions, or articulations, of the faith a Catholic has in God. Moreover, dogmatic statements are limited. They are limited for various reasons. First of all, they can only be partial expressions of the truths they are attempting to encapsulate because God is necessarily beyond our comprehension. If God exists at all, and of course Christians believe that he/she does exist, God's mode of existence is so different to ours that our understanding cannot encompass it.

But dogmas are also limited for a much simpler reason. As I said at the beginning of this Introduction, the Nicene creed was, for all but one short phrase, formulated in the fourth century. In the fourth century there were particular theological problems, and there were particular philosophical ways for tackling these problems. In other words, in order to understand the creed you have to know a great deal about the historical background from which it came. Dogmas themselves do not change: the truth to which they give expression remains always true. But that truth may be, and often is, rephrased, re-expressed, and thereby made more understandable to people of another, later generation. Moreover, because dogmas when first put down on paper are, as we have seen, necessarily limited, it may be that as time goes on Christians may be able to arrive at a better understanding of the truth which a dogma is expressing.

DENYING DOGMAS

Clearly, the ideas outlined briefly above, the Trinity and the Incarnation, are difficult to accept or to understand. Some people simply deny them, or they understand them in ways which may make them easier to grasp but which, in the thinking of the Church as a whole, do not adequately represent the truth as revealed in Scripture. Such people are, the Church would say, guilty of heresy – they are heretics. 'Heresy' comes from the Greek for 'choice', and has to be distinguished from 'Schism', from the Greek for 'tearing'. The former involves denial of a doctrine, the latter simply means separating oneself from the obedience to the Church, though in practice the words are often used interchangeably, particularly outside the Roman Catholic Church.

Heresies are important because, in practice, they help the Church to come to a clearer understanding of its doctrine. One of the early heresies, for example, was that of the priest Arius, who died in 336. The exact details of what he taught are uncertain, but what he was thought by his contemporaries to have argued was that God the Son was somehow subordinate to God the Father. If this were so, then humankind had not been redeemed by the eternal God but by one whom he had created, and that, in the thinking of the early theologians, would not do. Another, rather different, early heresy was that of Apollinarius, who died *c.* AD 390. Again it is unclear exactly what he taught, but it seems to have included the idea that Jesus did not have a human soul: the soul in Christ was the presence of God. But that meant that Jesus was not a proper human person, rather as Arius argued that Jesus was not properly God. There was a phrase, almost a slogan, of the early Christian writers (they are often referred to as 'the Fathers of the Church') that 'what has not been assumed by Christ is not redeemed'. Christ assumed, the argument ran, humanity in its totality, both body and soul. Therefore Apollinarius' version of Christ, a person without a human soul, did not express the truth about Jesus as the Church had come to understand it.

Though heretics were driven out of the Church if they remained firm in their opinions, debating with them helped Christian thinkers, or theologians, to clarify Christian doctrine. This is straying into the area which is properly covered by theology and philosophy, and something now has to be said about these two disciplines.

THEOLOGY AND PHILOSOPHY

The Greek word for God is 'theos', and 'logy' (also from the Greek) means 'the science of', or 'the study of'. So theology is the study of God and of God in his relation to the universe in general and to the human race in particular. There are various kinds of theology. There is, for instance, dogmatic theology or, as it is more often called nowadays, systematic theology, which deals with the dogmas of the faith in the sense in which we have just been considering them. It attempts to use whatever evidence we have to understand the dogmas better. And because dogmas are historically conditioned

statements, there is always something new to be said about them in successive generations. Then, to take another example, there is moral theology. This is concerned with humankind's relationship with God and with each other: how we behave towards God and how we behave towards one another.

But not only are there different branches of theology, there are different theologies, different ways of thinking. This is often because theologians have adopted different philosophies. Just as theology means the study of God, philosophy means the study of wisdom ('sophia' is Greek for wisdom), in other words the study of knowledge itself. There are different systems of philosophy, and when these are applied to religious data you get different sorts of theology.

There is no need to go any further into all this here, except to remark that some Christian Churches deny that one can use philosophy to get to a better knowledge of God: one has to rely solely upon the Scriptures. They argue this because they believe that, at the Fall, human nature was so thoroughly corrupted that human reason cannot come, by the power of reason alone, ever to know God. Human reason on its own cannot be trusted. Only reason based on revelation can be trusted. Catholics do not share that view. They have a more positive attitude to the potentiality of human reasoning, and have always applied philosophical thought to the understanding of the truths of the faith. The philosophy drawn from the writings of the medieval theologian Thomas Aquinas (1225–74) has had a special position in Catholic thought, but theologians down the centuries have used the philosophies of many diverse thinkers to good effect.

Philosophy and theology are both extremely important in understanding the intricacies of Roman Catholicism. But this book is about the basics, not about the intricacies.

WHAT THIS BOOK IS NOT

It is impossible to write about Catholicism, or indeed about Christianity in general, without going into some of the different theological positions adopted by different brands of Christianity. However, this book is not an attempt to persuade anyone of the truth – or otherwise – of the doctrines of Roman Catholicism in particular, or of Christianity in general. For instance, there is no

intention to defend the truth of any of the statements in the Nicene creed which have been discussed above. Nor is this book trying to defend Catholicism, except perhaps from some common misapprehensions. This book is meant to be an account, admittedly from an insider, of what Roman Catholicism is. It aims to be a description of what Catholics think and how they act, and to some extent of why they think and act the way they do.

There are any number of books which provide a defence of Roman Catholicism, or attempt to commend it as a faith to be followed. One recent book of this kind is *Catholicism: The Story of Catholic Christianity* by Gerald O'Collins and Mario Farrugia, full details of which (and of other books mentioned in the text) will be found in the Bibliography. This volume does an excellent job of portraying Roman Catholicism in both its historical context and its artistic context. Another book with a similar title, *Catholicism*, by Richard McBrien – a volume of well over 1,200 pages – gives a detailed treatment of the topics discussed in this book, and many more besides. Both these can in places be highly technical. Then there is The *Catechism of the Catholic Church*, which is an official statement of the faith, first published in 1992, and produced in an English translation two years later – though a revised edition was produced in English in 1999. A catechism traditionally teaches the faith by means of a question-and-answer method. While this latest one does not do this, it still presents Roman Catholicism in bite-sized sections, in nearly 3,000 numbered paragraphs.

In the 'Further Reading' sections at the end of each chapter these three volumes in particular will be referred to where appropriate, though mention will also be made of other books which may be of use, not all of them from Roman Catholic sources.

WHAT THIS BOOK IS

This book is an attempt to lay out the basics of Roman Catholicism in a systematic and logical fashion. This is not easy. The faith has developed as an organic whole. It is very difficult to discuss one bit of it without feeling constantly the need to cross-reference to other related bits. Cross-references do occur, but they have been kept to a minimum. The first part of the book deals with the structures of the Roman Catholic Church, the second part with beliefs and practices.

There is also, throughout, an attempt to answer frequently asked questions about the Church.

Chapter 1, therefore, deals rather generally with the existence of the Church in the world today, locating it within the wider body of Christianity. It deals with the question of how many Roman Catholics there are, and where the majority of them are to be found. As will be seen, it is a very large institution indeed, and this raises the issue of how it holds together. So the following chapter describes the various sources of authority within the Church. Roman Catholicism undoubtedly has some very distinctive beliefs and practices, but it is perhaps its centralised authority structure which most distinguishes it from other Christian Churches – indeed, from any other world faith.

The questions then naturally arise: who exercises this authority, over whom and how? Chapter 3 discusses the various categories of people within the Church, from the Pope to the people who turn up, Sunday after Sunday, for the religious service, but otherwise play little part in the official doings of Roman Catholicism. They are organised into parishes, dioceses and so on, and these structures constitute the subject of Chapter 4. It was remarked a moment ago that a distinguishing feature was the Church's central authority – the popes and the Vatican bureaucracy. The Vatican and its workings are described in Chapter 5, but to understand the papacy properly it is necessary to know something of its background. Hence a potted history of the popes has been added to the book as an Appendix.

The papacy is one of the most prominent features of Roman Catholicism, particularly since the accession of John Paul II in 1978. His extensive travels brought the centre of the Church, as it were, to the periphery. What Roman Catholics believe about the role of the papacy is considered in Chapters 4 and 5. But like most Christians, perhaps like most religious people, Roman Catholics reflect less on what they believe and more on what they do. The remaining chapters of the book consider their beliefs in the context of how they practise their faith.

Chapter 6 contains a long description of the central act of worship, the Mass, as well as the seven sacraments of the Church. There is in addition the formal prayer of the Church known as the Divine Office, to be said by all priests, monks and nuns. Some parts of it are also regularly recited by lay people as an act of devotion, and it is described in the following chapter, along with other, less formal devotions. This chapter also discusses the role of the 'religious', the monks and nuns (and others) just mentioned. The final chapter, Chapter 8, looks at the Church in the world, its ethical teaching on sexual morality as well as on issues of justice and peace, and it ends with a brief discussion of Liberation Theology – a recent movement in the Church which has arisen especially in the cultural context of Latin America, though it has also taken off elsewhere – which attempts to rethink the Roman Catholic Church's theology from the perspective of the marginalised in society.

SUMMARY

1   Roman Catholicism is a form of Christianity.
2   The beliefs of Christians, which Roman Catholics share, are summed up in creeds.
3   The chief beliefs, shared by all Christians, include:
   a   the Trinity
   b   the creation of the world by God
   c   the 'Fall' of Adam and Eve
   d   the incarnation of the Son of God
   e   the redemption.
4   Anyone who rejects a fundamental belief of Christianity separates him or herself from the Church and becomes a 'heretic'.
5   Discussion of these beliefs is called Theology.
6   This book is not as such a defence of Roman Catholicism, still less an attempt to convert anyone to the faith.
7   It is rather an attempt to describe the fundamental beliefs and religious activities of Roman Catholics, and to answer some of the questions which are most frequently asked about this branch of Christianity.

FURTHER READING

On the creed:

Kelly, *Early Christian Creeds* (a difficult but important book).

Young, *The Making of the Creeds*.

The *Catechism*, pp. 42–4.

On the Trinity, incarnation and redemption:

McBrien, *Catholicism*, chapters 7 and 12.

O'Collins and Farrugia, *Catholicism*, chapters 4 and 5.

The *Catechism*, pp. 49–156.

On theology:

McBrien, *Catholicism*, chapter 2.

1

THE CHURCH, CATHOLIC AND ROMAN

In the Introduction it has been seen that Roman Catholics profess the same creed as most other Christians. But does this make Roman Catholics Christians? While this may seem self-evident, it is a statement which, for different reasons, may be objected to both by some Roman Catholics and by some non-Catholics. This chapter will look at two things. First of all it will discuss the relationship between Roman Catholicism and worldwide Christianity, and then examine how the former exists in the modern world, its size and its geographical spread.

CHRISTIANITY

There are members of a number of Churches who wish to argue that very early on in its history the Catholic Church departed from the teachings of Jesus, the founder of Christianity, as those teachings have been preserved in the New Testament. They claim, for instance, that the institution of bishops (of course, to be found in other Churches as well as the Roman Catholic Church) is a deviation from the way the primitive Church was run, governed as it was by members of the local Christian community itself rather than by one man – the bishop – set over it. (The organisational structure adopted by Christian groups is often referred to as their 'Church polity'.) They are, therefore, particularly opposed to the claims of the Bishop of Rome – the Pope – to exercise authority over the whole Church. Christians who believe this are quite likely also to believe that only members of this 'primitive' version of the faith are going to be 'saved', that is, will go to heaven, and that Catholics most certainly do not qualify for salvation.

Catholics, on the other hand, argue that their Church is in direct line of continuity with the primitive Church, that institutions such as bishops developed within the lifetime of those who first had heard the message of Christ and, even if they are not expressly to be found in the New Testament, they are a logical organisational development and as such are implicit in God's plan for his Church. Some Catholics would go further. They argue that those who have, in Catholic eyes, separated themselves from God's Church and gathered in communities distinct from it, cannot constitute Churches themselves because there is only one Christian institution that can properly be called a Church, and that is the Roman Catholic one. In this view the Church Jesus founded, Christianity, is to be identified with the Roman Church, and with nothing that is outside it.

Both these views, either that the Roman Catholic Church is not Christian at all, or that, on the contrary, it is the one and only Christian Church, have their advocates. These are extreme positions. However, the belief that the Roman Catholic Church is the one, true, and only upholder of the faith taught by Jesus Christ was commonly held by Roman Catholics. In 1928 they were forbidden by an encyclical letter (see Box 1.1) of Pope Pius XI to involve themselves in any assemblies gathered to further the ecumenical movement – the movement, that is, to find common ground among the many Christian communities – precisely because they might thereby give the impression that there existed Christian truth outside the Catholic Church. (The term 'ecumenical' comes from a Greek word meaning 'of the whole world'.) By taking part in such meetings, said the Pope, the Catholic faith would be 'subverted by the desire of other Christians to treat the Catholic Church as one among many Churches'. There was only one way to achieve Christian unity, went on Pius XI, and that was for all other Christians to return to the Catholic Church.

BOX 1.1   PAPAL DOCUMENTS

An encyclical letter is a letter addressed to all Catholic bishops in the world. Encyclicals have been used with increasing frequency since they were re-introduced in 1740 as a means for the Pope to speak to the worldwide Church. They are named, as are most if not all documents issued by the Vatican, by the opening two or three words. These are usually in Latin, and are commonly untranslatable as titles because they only make sense within the complete (Latin) sentence. Thus the encyclical of Pius XI mentioned in the text, forbidding Catholics to engage in ecumenical activities, is called *Mortalium Animos*. In English it is some-times referred to a 'On fostering true religious unity', but that does not translate the Latin name. Perhaps the best known encyclical, that issued by Paul VI in 1968 condemning artificial means of contraception, is called *Humanae Vitae*, which can easily be translated as 'Of human life'. Sometimes, however, a vernacular (i.e., current, modern) language is used if it is more appropriate. Thus the encyclical of Pius XI issued in 1937 condemning Nazism was in German, and is known by its opening words in German: *Mit brennender Sorge* ('With burning anxiety').

TESTS OF CHRISTIANITY

But to return to the question of whether the Roman Catholic Church can be regarded as being Christian. There has been much time devoted by theologians to analysing Christianity in order to determine its 'essence', but to no great effect. A more pragmatic way of judging whether Roman Catholicism is Christian would be through its membership of the World Council of Churches (WCC). This organisation, based in Geneva, draws together very many Christian communities from around the world. It described itself, at its first General Assembly in Amsterdam in 1948, as 'a fellowship of Churches which accept our Lord Jesus Christ as God and Saviour'. This very simple statement was subjected to a good deal of criticism, and was reformulated in 1961 during the third General Assembly held in New Delhi. It now reads 'The World Council of Churches is a fellowship of Churches which confess the Lord Jesus Christ as God and Saviour according to the Scriptures and therefore seek to fulfil together their common calling to the glory of the one God, Father,

Son and Holy Spirit'. Membership of the WCC is restricted to bodies which can subscribe to this statement, and the statement is recognised as a (minimum) way of defining a Christian.

While the Roman Catholic Church would in principle have no difficulty signing up to such a statement, it is not in practice a member of the WCC. The reasons for this are in part historic. As has been explained above, the Church was initially hostile towards the burgeoning ecumenical movement, and forbade Catholics to become involved. That attitude has now very much changed, but there remain practical problems entailed in WCC membership. Perhaps the most obvious of these is the sheer size of the Roman Catholic Church. It is bigger than all other Christian bodies put together. It would therefore be unreasonable to treat it as just one among the other Churches. Other methods of membership have been canvassed: for example, entry of the Roman Catholic Church as national Churches (which is what many of the other members in practice are). But this would give it a predominant vote, should all the 'national' Roman Catholic Churches vote together, as well they might.

Another external criterion might be to take the statement of another body which is non-controversially Christian, and to judge Roman Catholicism against that. An appropriate one is the 'Lambeth Quadrilateral'. This statement of faith was drawn up originally for the Episcopal Church in the United States and agreed at a meeting in Chicago in 1886. The four points were to be the basic position to which any Church would have to subscribe if it wished reunion with the Episcopal Church. Two years later the Chicago formula was slightly revised and accepted by the Lambeth Conference, the gathering of all the Bishops of the Anglican Communion. The four points of the 1888 Lambeth Quadrilateral which would need to be accepted by any Christian Church seeking reunion with any member of the Anglican Communion – with the Church of England, for example – are:

> The Holy Scriptures of the Old and New Testaments as 'containing all things necessary to salvation', and being the rule and ultimate standard of faith.
> The Apostles' Creed, as the Baptismal Symbol ['Symbol' in this context is simply another word for creed], and the Nicene Creed, as the sufficient statement of the Christian faith.

The two sacraments ordained by Christ himself – Baptism and the Supper of the Lord – ministered with unfailing use of Christ's words of Institution, and of the elements ordained by him.

The Historic episcopate, locally adapted in the methods of its administration to the varying needs of the nations and peoples called of God into the Unity of his Church.

In 1920, when the Lambeth Conference issued an 'Appeal for Reunion' on the basis of these four points, it slightly altered the last one to make it rather more vague in its meaning. Even with its 'stronger' form of the final statement on bishops, the Roman Catholic Church would have no difficulty in signing up to the Lambeth Quadrilateral: it acknowledges the Scriptures, the creeds, the two sacraments and the institution of bishops as all being part of its own constitution. Of course, the statement is not an exhaustive set of criteria. The Roman Catholic Church, for instance, thinks there are seven, not two, sacraments. But certainly Baptism and the Lord's Supper – though it does not commonly use this expression – are among the seven. Of course, Roman Catholics do not understand statements like 'containing all things necessary to salvation' when referring to the Scriptures in quite the same way as members of the Anglican Communion would do (probably not all Churches within Anglicanism understand it the same way either), but they could certainly assent to it.

Enough has now been said to indicate that it is proper to include the Roman Catholic Church among the list of Christian Churches, and, as I suggested at the beginning, there are not many, though there may be some, who would deny it. The next point which has to be addressed is why the Roman Catholic Church calls itself both 'Roman' and 'Catholic'. It is easier to treat these terms in reverse order.

CATHOLIC

The word Catholic is an important term, and it is understood in a variety of ways. 'Catholic', for instance, is commonly contrasted to 'Protestant', where the latter expression refers to the Churches that sprang up at the Reformation. Protestant, historically, is a correct usage: the word was originally used in 1529 at the Diet of Speyer by those who were 'protesting' at the attempt to roll back the Reformation.

But that is not the whole story. The Lambeth Quadrilateral mentioned above lists adherence to the creeds as an essential part of the Anglican interpretation of the Christian faith. In the course of reciting those creeds, Christians, even distinctly Protestant Christians of the kind described who would have nothing at all to do with Roman Catholicism, profess their faith in the 'one, holy, *catholic* and apostolic Church'. So, confusingly, even Protestants lay claim to being Catholics. The creeds were, of course, written long before the divisions of Christendom into its various denominations or Churches. That, however, is not the point. The point is the fundamental meaning of the word 'Catholic'.

'Catholic' comes from a Greek word meaning universal, so it means the one Church, worldwide. Applied in this way to the Church, 'Catholic' is a very old usage. It can be traced back to the writings of Ignatius, who was Bishop of Antioch at the very end of the first and the beginning of the second centuries AD. He wrote: 'Where Jesus Christ is present, there we have the Catholic Church'. Ignatius was aware that there were a large number of local Christian communities: these were individual churches, but there was also a sense that there was only one church, the 'Catholic' church, of which these scattered communities were local instances. So one meaning of the word Catholic is that the Church is geographically universal.

The term can also mean true, or authentic, and in that sense it can be, and historically has been, applied to local Churches to indicate that they taught the fullness of doctrine, everything that was needed for salvation. So those Christian communities or, more often, individuals said to be heretical were heretical because they were not teaching the true faith: were not, in other words, Catholic.

There is a close link between the two meanings, universal and authentic. A community knows that its teaching is authentic – is Catholic – when such teaching is consonant with what is taught by the universal – Catholic – Church. This is an important principle in Christianity, and was soon recognised as such. It was summed up by Vincent of Lérins – Lérins is a small island off Cannes which is now known as St-Honorat, after the founder of the abbey at which

Vincent (*d.* before 450) was a monk – in what is known as the Vincentian Canon. When distinguishing true and false traditions within Christianity, wrote Vincent, the true one is that which had been believed 'everywhere, always, and by all'. 'Catholic', then, meant universal in time as well as in space.

So universal/authentic is the fundamental meaning of the word Catholic, and that is the sense in which it is used in the creeds. As no Christian would really want to say that his or her belief was inauthentic, did not represent the teaching of Christ, then all Christians can profess belief in the Catholic Church.

BOX 1.2   CHURCHES OF THE EAST IN COMMUNION WITH ROME

When 'Eastern' is used of Churches, it means those Churches whose origins lie in the Eastern capital of the Roman Empire, Constantinople, and in the Middle East – in Syria, Iraq, Jordan, Lebanon, Armenia and so on. Some of those Churches also became established very early on in India, probably through Syrian traders – though these Indian Christians themselves attribute their origins to St Thomas the Apostle.

However, as remarked above, 'Catholic' is regularly also used in opposition to 'Protestant', and it is also used in opposition to the term 'Orthodox', a term which many Churches of the East apply to themselves – the Greek Orthodox Church, the Russian Orthodox Church, and so on. The use of Catholic as opposed to Orthodox goes back to the separation between the Church of the West and that of the East, between Rome and Constantinople, which occurred definitively – the two had long been drifting apart – in 1054; Catholic as opposed to Protestant goes back to 1529 and the Diet of Speyer.

In common usage, however, the matter is not quite so straightforward. Some of the Churches which arose out of the sixteenth-century Reformation now think of themselves not as Protestant but as Catholic. They do so because the term 'Protestant' has come to mean a particular, radical, understanding of the Reformation, a decisive break with the tradition which went before. There are Christians outside Roman Catholicism who do not want to assert such a radical discontinuity both in faith and in practice. They are often quite similar in their beliefs and worship to Roman Catholics, and particularly in Church polity: Catholics in this sense will, again like Roman Catholics, always give a significant role to the office of bishop. Many members of the Church of England and of the Episcopal Church in the USA, and other members of the Anglican Communion in Africa and Asia, are Catholics in this sense.

Finally, there is a modern meaning given to the term 'Catholic' which has its roots in the original sense of universal. It arises from the missionary enterprise, and has always been present in Christianity though it has come to prominence relatively recently. The Church is Catholic, it is argued, because its message can be embodied in any of the very many diverse cultures it has encountered in the course of its history. In fact the degree to which the Christian message and its worship can be embodied – 'inculturated' is the usual term – in diverse cultures has frequently been a matter of dispute, certainly within the Roman Catholic Church.

WHY ROMAN?

As the previous section attempted to explain, the term 'Catholic' has so many meanings, and is claimed by so many different Churches, that it cannot properly be used (though of course in practice it is) to denominate one specific Christian community. The Christians commonly known as Catholics should more properly be known as Roman Catholics.

A good many Roman Catholics object to the epithet 'Roman'. They do so for a variety of reasons. One is linked to what was said in the first section, that they believe that they are the only true Church, therefore the only Catholic Church, and calling them Roman rather suggests that there are other, equally valid, kinds of Catholic, such as – and in particular – Anglo-Catholic. Another reason why the term is disliked is because it is sometimes used by those hostile to Roman Catholicism to suggest that its adherents do not really belong to the nation in which they live, that they are somehow 'foreign'. Some critics would go even further and claim that, because Roman Catholics owe some degree of obedience to the Pope, they cannot be loyal citizens of their native land. This was not an uncommon attitude, at least in Britain, from the late sixteenth to the late nineteenth centuries, and it has surfaced in the USA when there have been contenders to the presidential election who were Roman Catholics.

There is an additional sensitivity in Britain. In 597 the Roman monk Augustine arrived at the court of the pagan king Ethelbert in Canterbury. He had been sent by Pope Gregory I to convert the Anglo-Saxons to Christianity. This he and his successors achieved, and the ecclesiastical organisation of the Church of England still reflects the structure which he began to put in place. The coming of Augustine is sometimes referred to as the 'Roman mission', with the suggestion that the 'Roman' Catholicism which Augustine brought somehow drove out a purer, quasi-indigenous, Celtic Christianity which existed on the island of Britain prior to his arrival.

There is a sense in which it is true that a 'Roman' understanding of what the Church should be like eventually triumphed over a Celtic one. Celtic Christianity had developed in a world in which there were no major centres of habitation. It was therefore structured around monasteries, and this eventually gave way to the urbanised version of Church polity which Augustine brought with him. Another difference between the two versions of Christianity was the date on which the feast of Easter was to be celebrated. In 664, at the Synod of Whitby, it was decided to follow the Roman rather than the Celtic tradition for deciding the date of Easter. But it would be wrong to suggest that those following the Celtic practices and those following the Roman ones considered themselves as belonging to anything other than the Catholic Church – though the Celts might not have given it much thought.

Despite the Celtic experience, Christianity was, and still very largely is, organised around dioceses. 'Diocese' is a term which the Church took over from the Roman imperial government, where it meant a group of provinces into which the Empire was divided for administrative purposes. The local Christian community was not originally called a diocese but a 'Church', and later – and perhaps rather confusingly for us – a 'parish' – the term 'parish' is still used rather than diocese in the Eastern Church. The word diocese, meaning the geographical area under the control of a bishop, gradually began to replace the term parish from the fourth century onwards, and had done so more or less completely by the ninth century.

The diocese, or local Church, was commonly coterminous with a town or city, and there were a great many of them, each with a

CATHOLIC NUMBERS

That is, however, the case. There were estimated to be, in the year 2000, rather over 1.8 billion Christians. The SYB calculated that the Catholic population was slightly over 1.045 billion, of whom perhaps 18 million – a tiny proportion – belong to the non-Latin rites listed in the box on page 22. There are, of course, vastly more non-Christians than Christians. Christianity remains, however, the largest religious faith. Islam comes next: it has a larger number of adherents than does Catholicism, but it is, somewhat like Christianity, divided into groups which may be likened to denominations, none of which is as large as Catholicism. Both faiths, Islam and Christianity, are growing at roughly the same rate.

The SYB records the number of baptisms performed, which is a relatively safe statistic because they have all to be recorded. In the year 2000 there were rather more than 18 million baptisms, of which 2,718,044 (the figures seem remarkably precise) were of 'adults' – that is, in the Church's eyes, anyone over seven years of age. These presumably were mainly converts to the faith, and the majority of them were in Africa. But apart from baptism, there are two further stages in the initiation process, the reception of first communion, usually at the age of seven, and then of confirmation, which in normal circumstances can be at any age from seven or eight to fifteen and sixteen. The figures seem to indicate that only just over half those who are baptised proceed to the final initiatory step and are confirmed. The figure of 18 million or so baptisms has been reasonably stable over the past few years. It exceeds the death rate and suggests that Catholicism is still growing. On the other hand, the number of baptisms as a proportion of Catholics has been in decline, following the general trend in most countries of a decreasing birth rate. Catholics constitute just over 17 per cent of the total population of the world, a proportion that is steadily in decline, even though the number of Catholics is increasing.

As has already been said, Catholics are organised into 'dioceses' each with a Church official at its head. This 'official' is usually a bishop or an archbishop, but there is a range of other titles depending both on the status of the person and the rite to which he (and it is always a 'he') belongs. At the end of 2000 there were 202 'dioceses' belonging to the Eastern rites, and 2,644 belonging to the

bishop at its head. They knew they were part of the Catholic Church because the bishop was 'in communion' with his neighbouring bishops. This communion was demonstrated in various ways, for example by the exchange of letters. But when a new bishop had to be appointed, the links between the Churches was demonstrated by the neighbouring bishops gathering for the ceremony of consecration. Those bishops who could celebrate the liturgy together were 'in communion' with each other.

In the Roman Catholic Church the bishop with whom all its bishops are in communion is the Bishop of Rome, the Pope. Perhaps it would be better to describe the Roman Catholic Church as the 'Roman Communion' of Churches, because to call it Roman Catholic upsets a large number of Christians who are in communion with the Bishop of Rome, but are not in any other sense 'Roman' Catholics.

It has already been mentioned that in 1054 there occurred a formal separation of the Churches of the East, which tended to look for leadership towards Constantinople (the modern Istanbul), from the Church of the West, centred on Rome. Some of these Eastern Churches later entered once again into communion with the Church of Rome, while retaining their own form of liturgy, ecclesiastical discipline, governance and structures, and clerical dress. The most obvious distinction between these Churches and the Roman Catholic Church is the liturgy, which in the case of these Eastern-rite Churches was never Latin, as in the West, but in some other ancient language, Greek or Syriac, for example, or even Coptic. There are twenty-one of these Churches. They are in communion with the Church of Rome, but certainly cannot properly be described as Roman Catholic. They are not specifically discussed in this book, though they will occasionally be mentioned.

Their existence, however, poses a question: what should this Church, which has so far been discussed under the name the Roman Catholic Church, properly be called? Many Churches have a geographical designation – the Church of England, for example, or the Church of South India. The 'Roman' in the Roman Catholic Church's title, on the other hand, does not have a geographical meaning, but a liturgical one: there is the Roman rite (liturgy) which used to be in Latin but no longer is. (This is not strictly true: the liturgy still exists, and is occasionally celebrated in Latin, but

celebrated rarely enough not to contradict the general principle.)
We have, then, the Greek rite, the Syriac rite and the Roman rite,
among others, all part of the Catholic Church in communion with
the Bishop of Rome. The Latin, or Roman, rite Catholics are by far
the biggest group in the Church, but not the only group. From now
on, therefore, this book will talk about the Catholic Church, without
the additional epithet 'Roman', though it will normally be
discussing Roman, or Latin, rite Catholics.

BOX 1.3 EASTERN CATHOLIC CHURCHES

Name	Membership (to nearest thousand)
Albanian	Unknown
Armenian	143
Belorussian	30
Bulgarian	15
Chaldean	628
Coptic	167
Ethiopian	133
Greek	2
Hungarian	253
Italo Albanian	61
Krizevci	49
Malabar	2940
Maronite	2176
Melkite	1147
Romanian	1563
Russian	Unknown
Ruthenian	461
Slovak	400
Syrian	185
Syro Malankara	295
Ukrainian	4195

Although the Churches mentioned in the box are described as
'Eastern rite', the largest of them is in Europe, the Greek Catholic
Ukranian Church, and the next largest is the Malabar Church in
Kerala, India, followed by the Maronites mainly in the Lebanon.

But they are all relatively small. In comparison to the Latin
Church, indeed, they are tiny. It is to the numbers, and distributi
of the Western Catholic Church that we will now turn.

THE DEMOGRAPHY OF CATHOLICISM

Statistics of religious adherence are notoriously unreliable.
most obvious indicator of commitment, for example, is attenda
at a regular place of worship: Catholics will go to Cath
churches, Methodists to Methodist ones and so on. It sh
therefore be possible to count attendance on a particular day
decide how many people are Catholic, how many Methodist
so on. But it isn't quite that straightforward. Will any Sunda
for such a census? Obviously not, because a great many
people attend church on the great festivals – at Easter
Christmas, say – than on other Sundays in the year. The expe
attendance for Catholics at church is every Sunday: does g
less often than once a week rule you out as a Catholic? And if
how often do you have to attend to qualify as a Catholi
censuses or surveys people may put themselves down as 'R
'C. of E.', but rarely if ever go to church: should they be incl
in statistics? One other issue is rather less studied, but non
less important: how far can someone deviate from the core b
of the religion to which he or she claims to belong and still
as an adherent?

There are, then, a great many difficulties involved in addi
the numbers. Nevertheless, there are a number of attem
produce statistics, and, with the caveats given above, this s
and the next give some impression of the size and the locat
the global Catholic population. This task is made considerably
because the Vatican maintains a statistical office which publis
annual summary. And it is relatively up to date: the data re
in the *Annuarium Statisticum Ecclesiae* (*Statistical Yearbook*
Church or SYB) for the year 2002 reflects the situation at
of the year 2000. The statistical office does not go in for co
tive statistics: it provides figures only for the Catholic Cl
and, where significant, for a country's total population. But
not claim, for example, that the Catholic Church is the
largest Christian denomination.

Latin rite. These dioceses were then further divided into 408,637 parishes or quasi-parishes or some other form of mass-centre. Most of these would would be headed by a priest, but not all of them, especially in 'missionary' countries such as Africa, or where priests are scarce, such as in much of Latin America.

CLERGY NUMBERS

Catholics regard priesthood as a 'vocation' – literally, 'a calling'. The calling is by God to the individual, and then by the Church to the individual in accepting him for ordination. But the number of people responding to the call from God has been dropping. The number of clergy has been a matter of concern for some time, and there has been a good deal of pressure especially in Western Europe and North America for the ordination of women (of which more later), and for the relaxation of the requirement that priests remain unmarried (of which also more later) so that more clergy could be recruited.

The number of priests is indeed declining rapidly in both Western Europe and North America. The number of clergy in these areas is certainly going down, and going down quite dramatically – a loss of over 5,000 in five years in Western Europe and over a thousand in the USA; elsewhere in the world the number of clergy attached to dioceses is generally on the increase. Moreover, outside Europe and the USA the number of candidates for the priesthood is also going up. But the rise in diocesan clergy has been off-set by a worldwide decline in the number of clergy belonging to religious orders. The global total of priests has, therefore, remained relatively steady. There are, in total, just over a quarter of a million diocesan priests, and just over 132,500 priests who are members of religious orders, just about 400,000 Catholic priests in total. The percentage who die each year has been steadily going up, however, reflecting the age profile of the clergy.

As has been said, the decline in the number of clergy, and the drop of new recruits to the rank of the clergy, has been greatest in Western Europe. As a result there has, over the past five years, been a substantial reduction in the number of parishes – by nearly 8,000. There has also been a decline, though a less significant one, in the USA. For the most part, however, the trend has been the other way, even in areas such as Central and South America where hitherto there has been a constant shortage of clergy.

But this rather crude statistic disguises a multitude of variations. If you calculate the ratio of priests to Catholics in the different areas of the world a very different picture emerges. In Central America there is one priest to rather more than 8,000 Catholics, in South America one to just over 7,000. These figures obviously reflect the large Catholic populations of these regions. In Africa there is one priest to every 4,700 or so Catholics. In North America and Western Europe, where, as we have seen, the decline is the greatest, there are still only just over 1,300 Catholics to every priest. Not surprisingly, therefore, parishes in Europe cater for a relatively small number of Catholics, less than 2,000 people each. Consequently the dioceses in Europe cover a smaller area than anywhere else. The typical diocese in Africa is more than five times the size of a European one.

As was remarked at the beginning of this section, it is important to treat statistics such as these with some caution. Taken at their face value, they show that Mongolia and Algeria are among the countries in the world with the best ratio of Catholics to priests. But that, of course, is because there are so few Catholics. One of the worst ratios, on the other hand, is to be found in Angola, where Portugese colonial rule left behind a great many Catholics but very few clergy to serve them. So this leads on to the question, where are most Catholics to be found?

THE GEOGRAPHY OF CATHOLICISM

The distribution of Catholicism does indeed reflect the various countries' colonial pasts. In Angola, for example, just over half the citizens are Catholics, and the same is true of the Congo's very much larger population – the Congo was, of course, colonised by Catholic Belgium. But the most significant Catholic population is to be found in Latin America, colonised by Spain and Portugal. Latin America is home to almost exactly half the world's Catholics. Non-Catholic denominations have made some inroads into the traditional Catholic hegemony of the region, but the numbers still remain immense. Brazil is the world's most populous Catholic country, with a total population of nearly 170 million, of whom

Catholics account for over 140 million: there are more Catholics in Brazil than in the whole of Africa. The next most populous Catholic country is Mexico, with over 89 million Catholics out of a total of just over 97 million.

Colonisation does not account for the whole story. The Philippines, once occupied by Spain, has some 62 million Catholics; the USA, never a colony of a Catholic regime, has rather more, amounting to nearly a quarter of its population. Over 90 per cent of the people of tiny East Timor, with its Portugese past, are Catholic, whereas only just about 2 per cent of the people of India are Christians at all. Given India's former colonial ties to Britain, one might have expected the greater proportion of these to be Anglicans, but in fact the greater proportion – over 16 million – are Catholics.

The figures given in this chapter are for baptised Catholics. That does not imply that they are attending church regularly, or indeed at all. France is one of the least religiously observant countries of Europe, yet nearly 80 per cent of its population have been baptised. Baptism rates remain high in countries with a Catholic heritage, but practice rates vary enormously. As has already been said, these statistics have to be handled with caution. They are given here only as a general indication of the spread of Catholicism around the globe.

Catholicism is, then, a very large Church indeed, and very widespread. And that gives rise to the question, what holds it all together? Why do different parts of it not divide off into separate Churches? The answer to that is to be found in the Catholic attitude to authority, and it is that to which the next chapter is devoted.

SUMMARY

1 Roman Catholicism is part of the Christian faith, though this is sometimes challenged by:
    a   some extreme groups outside the Church who deny it is Christian;
    b   some extreme groups within the Church who deny those outside it can be truly Christian.
2 It is true it is not a member of the World Council of Churches, but could none the less sign up to the WCC's (and others') fundamental statements of Christian belief.

3   The Roman Catholic Church is a communion of Churches who are all linked especially through the Bishop of Rome (the Pope).

4   Some members of the Church object to the word 'Roman' in its title for a variety of different reasons, not least because it makes the Church sound somehow 'foreign'.

5   Others are unhappy with the term because they belong to the Eastern Churches with a distinct history and discipline, and whose ties with Rome are very different from those of the Western Churches.

6   ;The expression 'Catholic' will therefore be used in this book, rather than 'Roman Catholic'.

7   The Catholic Church is by far the largest form of Christianity, and for the most part is still growing outside North America and Western Europe.

8   It is, however, suffering from a steep decline in the numbers of the clergy.

9   It can be found all over the world, particularly in those territories (Latin America in particular) which were colonised by Catholic powers.

FURTHER READING

McBrien, *Catholicism*, pp. 3–8.

The *Catechism*, pp. 192–5.

Annuarium Statisticum Ecclesiae (SYB).

Barrett, *World Christian Encyclopedia*, passim.

Fahlbusch, *The Encyclopedia of Christianity* (see under names of countries).

Smart, *Atlas of the World's Religions*, pp. 166–7.

2

AUTHORITY

While Catholics frequently distinguish between authority as such and the manner in which it is exercised, they have no doubt that it is necessary for the Church. Nor, for that matter, for Christians as a whole; but, as will be seen, Catholics rather differ from other Christians about where it is located, and have really quite a strong view of authority. The stress on authority is in fact one of the distinguishing features of Catholicism.

All authority, political as well as religious, comes from God, but obviously has to be exercised in this world by human beings. But this means, in the Christian view of things, all those who exercise authority have a responsibility, and will be answerable, to God for the manner of its exercise. It is also a service. That is to say, it is not exercised for the benefit of those in authority but for the benefit of those over whom it is exercised.

There is a good deal about authority and its close relative power in the Scriptures, especially in the New Testament. Jesus taught as one in authority (Mk 1:22), and he passed that authority on to his closest followers, the apostles, especially the authority to spread his teaching (Mt 10:7, Mt 28:18–20, Mk 16:15–16). Even Jesus's authority, however, was that of one who serves (Luke 22:27).

TRADITION

That authority is essential to the Church has been accepted even from the earliest years of Christianity. It was the main point of the First Letter of Clement of Rome, the earliest Christian document to have survived outside the New Testament (though, like the New Testament, it was at least in some places read aloud during the liturgy). A Clement is included in the succession lists of the bishops of Rome (see the section on the papacy), but whether the Clement of the First Letter is the same one is debatable since it was a fairly common name. Whatever his status, Clement wrote the letter around the year AD 96 as if he were a secretary to the (or a) Christian community in Rome. It was addressed to the Christians of Corinth, and it reads as if the Corinthians had asked for Rome's intervention in a dispute which was dividing their Church. The exact nature of the dispute is unclear, but the senior members of the community, called presbyters (a word which means 'elders'), had been ousted from office. Clement rebuked those who had taken part in this action, regarding it as the overturning of traditional authority.

AD 96 may seem rather soon to be talking of 'traditional authority', but Clement is quite clear. 'Tradition' is something handed on, and that is precisely what Clement described: Christ handing on the message to his apostles, and the apostles to those whom they appointed, bishops and priests and so on. Those who had received this teaching have the responsibility, and the authority, to hand on the faith which they had been taught by the apostles who in turn had been taught by Christ. At one point Clement calls those in authority 'rulers' of the Church, and it is clear that one of their functions was to preside at the liturgy. Authority, therefore, lies in the hands of those commissioned to preserve the teaching of Christ, and to hand it on.

THE CHURCH

The Church, then, is the repository of this tradition. 'Church' is a tricky term. The word itself comes from the Greek term *ekklêsia*, in the Romance languages by way of the Latin equivalent *ecclesia* (*église* in French, for example, or *iglesia* in Spanish), in English, German and Dutch it still comes from the Greek but via a Germanic root. *Ekklêsia* is the term used in the New Testament primarily for the Christian assembly, the gathering of Christians in a particular place (first-generation Christians seem consciously to have avoided using the equivalent Jewish term 'synagogue'). However, the later writings of the New Testament appear to apply *ekklêsia* universally, and not just to a gathering in a particular place.

This shift of usage is still reflected in the whole manner of different ways the word 'Church' is used by Catholics. The most obvious use, of course, is to refer to the building in which the liturgy is performed. In this book such usage is indicated, when it occurs, by spelling the word with a lower-case 'c' – 'church'. But the word can also indicate either the whole Christian body or just the Catholic portion of it, according to context. One can also say 'the Church in England' (rather than the Church of England), again meaning either the whole Christian body in England, or just the Catholics. A further meaning indicates the hierarchy, the authority structures that is, as opposed to the ranks of the non-ordained or laity. Sometimes in this context it includes all the clergy, as distinct from the laity, from priests to pope, sometimes – perhaps more frequently – the bishops as a group (the hierarchy), sometimes the Vatican and its bureaucracy. In this book I will use Church, with a capital 'C', to mean the whole Catholic body, priests and lay people.

BOX 2.1   THE CATHOLIC HIERARCHY

'Hierarchy' comes from two Greek words, and literally means 'rule by priests'. It has long been used to indicate the structure of government within the Catholic Church.

The common perception of the hierarchy puts the Pope at the top, followed by certain senior bishops called Cardinals, a rank 'below' cardinals called archbishops, then bishops and finally priests. As this book progresses it will become clear that the hierarchical structure is not a simple pyramid as this description might seem to indicate.

Catholics sometimes use other terms to refer to the Church. Two of the most common are 'the mystical body of Christ' and 'the people of God'. The former has its origin in the New Testament, though without the adjective 'mystical' (the 'mystical body' in

Christian writings until the middle ages meaning the Eucharist); the latter traces its roots to the Old Testament, which records the Israelites being chosen as God's own people, and entering into a covenant, or agreement, with him.

MODELS OF THE CHURCH

As with all 'models', the two images express slightly different though complementary ideas. In the context of the Church's authority, the 'body of Christ' image is perhaps the more important, and the most significant passage about it in the New Testament appears in Paul's letter to the Colossians (1:8): Christ 'is the head of the body, the Church'. The Church, therefore, as a whole continues to represent Christ in and to the world, so it represents the authority which Christ had from God (in Christian theology, of course, which Christ had from his Father, Christ also being divine). Christ's authority, which resides in the Church, is exercised most frequently by individuals (bishops, priests), and rarely if ever by the Church as a whole, just as, in a democracy, authority ultimately lies with the people but in the instance of a parliamentary democracy is exercised by the people's elected representatives.

The term 'mystical body of Christ' was given renewed prominence by the 1943 encyclical of Pope Pius XII, *Mystici Corporis Christi* ['Of Christ's mystical body']. The image of 'the people of God' was revived in particular by *Lumen Gentium* ['The light of the nations'], the document on the Church of the Second Vatican Council. It presents a rather more dynamic image than does 'the mystical body', and suggests a Church 'on the move' – appropriately, as its origins of the term lie in the liberation of the Jews from Egypt and their conquest of the Promised Land. The promised land for the Church, however, is the coming of the Kingdom of God, which is not achievable in this world, but to which the Christian people must strive. The 'people of God' motif, then, has inspired a rather more political, activist vision of the Church. This has caused some alarm in the Vatican, and there have been warnings against the misuse of the expression by the Church's International Theological Commission in 1984, and the following year by the Synod of Bishops.

'Models' of the Church were mentioned a moment ago. In 1974 an American Jesuit theologian – and later Cardinal – Avery Dulles published *Models of the Church*. In it he distinguished a number of different models, arguing that no single one of them responded adequately to the reality of the Catholic Church, but that each of them individually gave you a picture of what it ought to be and how it ought to operate. The models he puts forward are these:

1   the institutional model: the structured Church with its office holders exercising authority within it;
2   the community model: the Church's members being united with each other and united with God;
3   the sacramental model: the Church as a worshipping community and a sign to all of God's grace and offer of redemption;
4   the kerygmatic model: the Church as a means to bring the world to the knowledge of Christ and his mission of redemption (the word 'kerygma' means preaching, proclaiming Christ's message, rather than formal doctrinal instruction);
5   the servant model: the Church as a means of transforming the world and inculcating in society – in this instance by the actions of its members rather than by preaching as in 4 above – the values of the kingdom of God;
6   the disciple model: the Church as a community of disciples (which Dulles added later, and is a variant of 2 above).

As Dulles remarked, no one model exhausts the concept of the Church as understood by Catholics, but taken together they give some sense of the different ways in which members of the Church interpret their adherence to Catholicism. There are those, for example, who put greatest emphasis on the first model, that of the Church as an institution, and they will talk about the rules of belonging, and how one might find oneself outside the 'club'. This sort of model was in the ascendency before the Second Vatican Council – indeed, for many ordinary Catholics as distinct from the professional theologians it was, perhaps, the only model.

Just what the structures of the Church are will be described later in this chapter and in the next, but it is important to remember that, for Catholics, whatever the 'model' which most expresses their own understanding, the Church is both a *structured* society and at a same time a worshipping *community*. Moreover it is both international and local. It is the act of worship, the Mass or Eucharist, which is the source of unity in the Church. When it is said, for instance, that the Bishop of Rome is 'in communion with' the Archbishop of Westminster, say, or of New York or of Santiago de Chile or of Harare, it means quite literally that he would celebrate the Eucharist with them, give them communion, or receive communion from them. This point is graphically illustrated at the ordination of a new bishop, because several bishops will join him at the altar to celebrate the Eucharist. It is a sign of the Church's unity.

SCRIPTURE

It is odd that the Scriptures, which all Christians acknowledge as the foundation documents of their faith, should be a source of division rather than of unity in Christianity. But it is none the less the case. A non-Catholic, writing a similar book to this, would very likely have reversed the order of this section and the previous one. He or she would have put the Scriptures before the Church as a source of authority – perhaps as the only source of authority. He or she would argue, quite rightly, that the Bible is the word of God himself, and must be obeyed before all other authority.

But this statement is not as simple as it at first sight appears. All Christians believe that God reveals, or communicates, himself to human beings through his acts in history which have been recorded in what are called the Old and the New Testaments. Problems arise, however, in three ways.

1   If it is God's self-communication, is this limited to the two Testaments, or are they somehow only a privileged form of that self-communication?
2   How was this self-communication made known to and recorded by those who wrote it down in the books of the Bible?
3   Which books in fact carry this record?

Question 1 is much debated nowadays. Some Christians claim to have 'private' revelations, but these are, on the whole, ignored by the official Church. More problematic is the relationship – if any –

between the Christian Scriptures and the Scriptures of other religions. In what sense do the Koran, or the Hindu Scriptures, contain 'revelation'? To discuss this would be to stray far from the central theme of this book, and in any case there is no 'basic' attitude among Catholics, any more than there is among other Christians.

Question 2 divides some Christians, variously called Evangelicals or Fundamentalists, from Roman Catholics because Catholics are prepared to say, with others, that, although the Scriptures contain the self-communication of God, the texts were written down at particular times and places by people who were thoroughly immersed in the cultural milieu of their own time and place. The Scriptures contain messages which are of perennial significance, alongside details that were relevant only at the time the books were written. In order to understand them properly one has to study the context in which they were written, and the specific purpose, at that time, for which they were written. The Scriptures are the word of God, but they have been conveyed in the words of men.

This means, of course, that there is plenty of room for interpretation, to decide what the scribes were trying to say. And there was also plenty of room for the scribes to get things wrong – not, a pious Catholic would say, in communicating the message of God, but in the incidentals to that message. To take an obvious example: at the very beginning of the Bible the scribe writing down the account of creation said it occurred in seven 'days'. No one, I think, nowadays thinks the word 'day' means a period of twenty-four hours. There are, however, Christians who believe that God created everything at the beginning of time, and that evolution is not just a theory but a myth. Catholics do not have a problem in understanding the account in the Book of Genesis as itself a 'myth', a way of describing God's responsibility for the act of creation without committing oneself to the story as an historical 'fact' – whatever 'history' might mean so far back at the beginning of time.

It has to be admitted that Catholics were not always quite so relaxed about the Bible. There was certainly a time when the theory of evolution was frowned upon, and the means of interpreting the Bible suggested above, which are now commonplace, were also disapproved of. This period lasted, in broad terms, from the middle of the nineteenth century to the middle of the twentieth.

As late as 1950 the Pope was insisting that Adam and Eve were real people. Before the mid-nineteenth century a more literal (or 'fundamentalist') understanding of the Scriptures was rather taken for granted by all Christians. Occasionally this attitude gave rise to problems. The case of Galileo is notorious. Early in the seventeenth century he was condemned by the Pope of the day for teaching that the earth goes round the sun, because this contradicted the Bible as it was then interpreted. (Perhaps it ought to be remarked that the system Galileo was espousing is known as the Copernican system, named after Nicolaus Copernicus, who was himself a priest.)

The beginning of the freedom which Catholic scholars now enjoy in the use of scientific methods of biblical criticism and interpretation can be dated quite precisely. It began when, on 30 September 1943, Pope Pius XII issued an encyclical – a letter to all the bishops of the Catholic Church – on understanding the Scriptures. It is called in Latin *Divino afflante Spiritu* ['The inspiration of the Holy Spirit'].

It has just been remarked that Catholic scripture scholars differ from fundamentalists over the interpretation of the Bible. But there is another, even more basic, distinction. Our knowledge of Christ comes mainly from the four 'lives' of Christ (they are not really biographies in the modern sense, hence the inverted commas) which we call the Gospels. The first three to be written – those of Matthew, Mark and of Luke – are called 'the synoptic' gospels, which means that they are clearly related to one another, and are telling the same story though from slightly different angles and with different purposes. How exactly they are related to one another remains a matter of debate. The gospel attributed to St John, sometimes known as the Fourth Gospel, is quite different from the others and, it is generally agreed, was written somewhat later.

Exactly when the gospels were written is still unclear, but it was probably between about AD 60 and 100. One thing is obvious: they were not written down during Jesus's own lifetime. They were constructed from stories and memories, more or less remote, that the first Christians passed on. These stories were part of the 'tradition' (the word means 'handed down') which the earliest followers of Jesus passed on to those who came after. What Catholics would argue, therefore, is that it was the Church which produced the Gospels. The Church, the Christian community or communities (it is evident that the gospels were written for different groups of Christians, with different backgrounds) came first, the New Testament as a series of written documents came afterwards.

THE CANON OF SCRIPTURE

This does not mean the Scriptures lack authority. Quite the contrary. They are, as it were, the foundation documents of the Church. They record the experience of the first generation of Christians. They are sacred texts, because they recount the life, death and resurrection of Christ, and Christ, Catholics (along with all Christians) believe, is the definitive revelation of God. But they are, as was said a few moments ago, the word of God in words of men. We need to employ all our scientific and literary skills to understand them properly.

This brings us to Question 3 in the list above: what precisely constitutes the 'them' of the previous sentence? Because Christianity is in direct line of descent from Judaism, it embraces the Hebrew Scriptures, which Christians call the Old Testament, as well as the Gospels and selected writings of first-generation Christians such as Paul. The books which go to make up the Christian Scriptures are known as 'the canon' of Scripture. The word 'canon' comes from a Greek word meaning measuring standard, or norm, and the books of the Scripture included in the canon are regarded as authoritative, or normative, for the faith, and in some sense (there is debate about this as about so much else) the inspired word of God.

How the canon of Scripture came to be the way it is, why some books were included and others not, is a complicated story – much more complicated for the Old Testament than for the New because about the latter there is no disagreement among Christians. In the earliest centuries, however, there was doubt about some of the books now included; the Letter to the Hebrews, for instance, which was originally attributed to Paul but was quite soon thought – rightly – not to be by him and therefore somewhat dubious. There was also a tendency in these early years to include some books not now accepted as canonical – the second-century *The Shepherd* by someone called Hermas, for example. But the list as we have it today had come into being by the middle of the fourth century.

To understand how the Old Testament canon came into being it is necessary to distinguish between two versions of the Old Testament. That which was used by the early Christians is called The Septuagint, from the Latin word for 70. There was a tradition that the Bible had been translated into Greek in Alexandria by 70 (or 72) Jewish scholars or rabbis. But it was not just a translation from the Hebrew Bible, it both changed the order of the texts, and included books which had been written in Greek that do not appear as part of the Hebrew canon.

In the sixteenth century some reformers, thinking to return to a closer understanding of the word of God, turned to the Hebrew Bible and away from the Septuagint. The books in the Greek version which are not in the Hebrew came to be called 'the Apocrypha'. 'Apocryphal' literally means 'hidden things', but it has come to mean fictitious, which the books of the Apocrypha certainly were not. Indeed, some of them are important witnesses to the history of the Jewish people in the last centuries before Christ. Nowadays, therefore, Scripture scholars prefer to use the term 'deuterocanonical' rather than 'apocryphal'. Because the Reformers had rejected the deuterocanonical texts, the Church, at a Council held in Trent in Italy in 1546, decided to declare once and for all what was the Scriptural canon of the Catholic Church.

One other important decision about the Bible was made at that Council. They declared that the definitive Latin text of the Scriptures – Latin, of course, being the language of the liturgy and of general communication within the Church at that time – was to be a translation known as the Vulgate. This translation had originally been made largely by St Jerome at the end of the fourth century, but over the hundreds of years of manuscript transmission the text had become corrupted. In the aftermath of the Council of Trent it was revised and for centuries became the standard version of the Bible for Catholics. Until the encyclical of Pius XII just mentioned, all translations into modern languages had to be made on the basis of the Vulgate, rather than from the more original Hebrew or Greek.

The adoption of the Septuagint rather than the Hebrew version of the Bible, and the insistence at Trent that translations could only be made on the basis of the Vulgate, effectively meant that

Catholics used a different version of the Bible from non-Catholics (though unsurprisingly – because after all they used Greek rather than Latin – Orthodox Christians also accepted the Septuagint collection of writings). Nowadays, however, there exist versions of the Bible which are common to both Catholics and Protestants.

What has been said about the way the Scriptures were created and handed down the generations of Christians gives rise to a number of problems. Clearly, it had to be decided which books were canonical and which were not. The question then arises who decided, and by what authority. The Church needed to be able to guarantee the authenticity of the teachings of Christ as they were recounted in the texts we have just been discussing. Where did the authority of the decision-makers come from?

APOSTOLIC SUCCESSION

Even in the earliest Christian writers, from the end of the first century AD, this presented itself as an issue to be discussed. They agreed that the faith had to be handed on, so the line of transmission from Peter and the other Apostles who had surrounded Christ was something which they took very seriously. This is what is known as the Apostolic Succession, the notion that there is an unbroken tradition from the Apostles down to the present day. In other words, the bishops of the Church stand in direct line of succession to the Apostles. This is meant in a very physical, realistic manner, in the sense that a modern bishop was created bishop by an existing bishop, who in turn was created bishop by someone else, who could theoretically trace the inheritance of his office right back to the time of the Apostles. Thus a bishop's authority to teach, and to ordain priests to carry on the Church's mission and life, stems directly from his (very) distant link with the Apostles.

This means, of course, that the Apostles themselves have to be understood in some sense as bishops – which is rather anachronistic because we know that the office of bishop as it came to be understood did not exist in New Testament times. However, there is a tradition that some of the Apostles established bishoprics, St Peter first at Antioch in Syria and then at Rome, and it is claimed that St Mark – admittedly, not technically an Apostle but an Evangelist (that is to say, a writer of a Gospel) – founded the Church in

Alexandria. The apostolic origin claimed for some bishoprics, Jerusalem, Antioch, Alexandria and Rome, gave them from the beginning a particular eminence in the wider Christian Church. Constantinople, the capital city of the Roman Empire in the East, later also claimed a similar eminence, a claim which was much disputed on the grounds that it did not have an apostolic foundation: it later acquired the supposed relics of St Andrew to provide it with the necessary apostolic legitimacy.

But if a bishop's legitimate authority rests upon this direct descent from the Apostles, it is easy to see that the Church is on very shaky ground: how can we know that a particular line of descent is valid in every single case? And if somewhere in the distant past the links went wrong, then there must be a very considerable knock-on effect down to the present day.

There are some people who still assert the most basic view of Apostolic Succession, namely that the physical link between a bishop and one or other of the Apostles exists. The Church itself, however, is rather more circumspect. It nowadays insists that the *college* of bishops, i.e. all the bishops of the Church taken together as a group, stands in succession to the *college* of the Apostles. This gets away from the problem of trying to establish every individual case of Apostolic Succession.

So Catholics believe – and, it should be said, not just Catholics – that the authenticity of the Faith is guaranteed by the Apostolic Succession as manifested in the college of bishops. For the most part the Church does not need the college as such to meet: individual bishops in their own area of jurisdiction, their diocese in other words, should be able to guarantee the teaching that is being handed down in their diocese as authentic. But sometimes there are disputes between bishops about the authenticity of a particular bit of doctrine, and the college has to come together to decide what is the correct interpretation. The bishops then meet in what are called Councils of the Church.

COUNCILS OF THE CHURCH

The sense of 'community' which underlies Catholicism has been mentioned before. It is not a 'gathered' Church, i.e. a Church whose individual members respond to a personal call. Rather it is first and foremost a community into which one is born, or which one joins. It is this community as a whole which has handed down the tradition received from the Apostles. This sense of belonging together as a community or 'people' goes back to the early Church – theologians would say goes back to Christ himself, who chose twelve Apostles consciously to mirror the twelve tribes which made up the people of Israel. One of the ways this community aspect is expressed is through meetings of the Church leaders, the bishops. We know that these occurred very early on in the life of the Church, though before the Roman Empire became entirely safe for Christians the meetings were usually fairly local – provincial Councils. These localised Councils, incidentally, continue to be held to deal with local problems, or formulate local policy. The bishops of England and Wales meet regularly, for instance, and so do those of the United States and of most nations with a large enough group of bishops: the largest of these 'bishops' conferences', as they are known, is that of Brazil. More formal meetings are sometimes called 'synods', which is simply a Latinised form of the Greek word for Councils. But these Councils legislate, if they legislate at all, only for local problems, not for issues affecting the Church worldwide. What we are concerned with here are Councils of, or more correctly for, the whole Church.

If in the middle of the twentieth century you had asked a Catholic about Church councils, he or she might very well have said that the age of councils was over because now the Pope had all authority to decide everything. The reason for saying that would, paradoxically, have been the decision of a Church council which, in 1870, had declared the Pope to be infallible when teaching the faith. Infallibility means that the Pope could not make a mistake about what Catholics ought to believe. And then, soon after he was elected in 1958, Pope John XXIII summoned another Council, known as the Second Vatican Council – or more commonly as Vatican II – which had an enormous impact not just upon the Catholic Church but on a great many people of other faiths. Vatican II rather goes against the definition implied above, that a Council meets to decide matters in dispute among bishops. There was nothing specifically in dispute – though it rapidly became clear in the course of the Council that there were after all many disagreements within the Church which needed to be settled.

Still, Vatican II is something of an exception. Councils have generally met to decide matters of doctrine or, sometimes, important matters of internal Church discipline (many, perhaps most, Councils have actually tackled both sets of issues). Councils, at least those which claim to represent the whole Church and are therefore known as 'ecumenical' (see p. 13 for the meaning of 'ecumenical') are regarded as the highest authority in the Church, and their decrees are binding on all. A list of them, with their dates, is given in the accompanying box. As can be seen, they take their names from the cities where they met – or, when they met in Rome, from the place in which the meetings were held, in one of the two basilicas (major churches), either St John Lateran or St Peter's in the Vatican.

BOX 2.2 COUNCILS OF THE CHURCH

Name	Date
Nicaea I*	325
Constantinople I*	381
Ephesus*	431
Chalcedon*	451
Constantinople II*	553
Constantinople III*	680–81
Nicaea II*	787
Constantinople IV	869–70
Lateran I	1123
Lateran II	1139
Lateran III	1179
Lateran IV	1215
Lyons I	1245
Lyons II	1274
Vienne	1311–12
Constance	1414–17
Basle Florence	1431–45
Lateran V	1512–17
Trent	1545–63
Vatican I	1869–70
Vatican II	1962–65

* Accepted as ecumenical by all Churches, both East and West

Although they are called 'ecumenical' by Catholics, they certainly did not represent the whole Church, at least in terms of numbers. Until the modern Councils, those called Vatican I and Vatican II, the number of bishops attending varied, but was usually a fairly small proportion of all those in the Church. In the earliest Councils which met in the East, there was only a small presence from the Western Church, and the Pope was not necessarily represented by bishops. None the less, the first seven Councils listed are regarded by most Christians (some non-Catholics do not accept the authority of Councils at all) as truly ecumenical. The eighth Council is not accepted as ecumenical by the Eastern Church (now called the Orthodox Church), nor any further Councils, because the Eastern and Western Churches formally condemned each other in 1054, and there could be no more Councils which truly represented the whole, united Church. (The eighth Council, it is true, preceded this division, but nevertheless it is not accepted in the East.)

After the division – or schism, to use the ecclesiastical term – between East and West, the Western Church continued to hold Councils, whose status may have been rather unclear to people of the time but are now by Roman Catholics usually counted among the ecumenical Councils. It might, however, be better to call them 'general councils'. Since the sixteenth century and the further division of the Church between Protestants and Catholics, there have been three Councils, still usually referred to as 'ecumenical', but which represent an even smaller proportion of the Church. It has been suggested by Dr Norman Tanner, who has made a special study of conciliar history and texts, that they be called 'general Councils of the Roman Catholic Church'.

Whatever the correct title for these Councils, the authority of them all is, for Catholics, the same. Catholics treat their decisions as equally binding, at least in principle. Here, however, the distinction between disciplinary decrees of Councils and their doctrinal ones is important. Disciplinary ones were usually addressed to particular situations which may no longer prevail, or may now present themselves very differently. Doctrinal decrees, say on the nature and person of Christ, were proclaimed to be true for all time. Even with these, however, one has to be careful. The texts of the Councils, at least up to the Council of Trent, have been transmitted by manuscripts, so there is a problem of establishing the correct version of what the Council 'fathers' decided. More importantly, people expressed themselves in the language and thought-patterns of their own day: we have to understand this – and them – if we want to be clear about what they were saying. Interpreting the Councils, in other words, is rather like interpreting the Scriptures.

None of these Councils has ever been attended by all the bishops of the whole Christian Church. The vast majority of the bishops of the Catholic Church came to Vatican II, but that was the exception: the number turning up has usually been only a small proportion of those eligible to attend. The Council of Trent, so called from the city of Trento in Northern Italy where it met for the first time in 1545, managed to gather only twenty-one bishops, four archbishops and a single cardinal, plus a handful of other clerics, for its opening session. There were more at later sessions, but even so the majority were from Italy and scarcely represented the worldwide Catholic Church. Still, it was recognised as a properly constituted Council by the Catholic Church, and its decrees have had an enormous influence on both the structure and the doctrine of the Church. It has just been remarked, for instance, that it was not until Trent that the canon of Scripture was formally decided, a millennium and a half after the last books of the New Testament had been written.

The rules which govern Councils have been laid down by the law of the Church, the canon law, of which more in a moment. It states, for instance, that only bishops have the right (and obligation) to attend and to vote, and that it must be called by the Pope. But in the first millennium Councils were certainly not always called by the Pope, though when he was not represented he gave his approval afterwards to the deliberations and decisions. And they have certainly not always been limited to bishops. The Council of Constance, for instance, was rather dominated by the Emperor Sigismund who called it; the Pope of the day only reluctantly agreed, guessing, as indeed turned out to be the case, that the Council would demand his resignation.

COUNCIL OVER POPE?

This raises for Catholics the fundamental question of whose authority is the greater, that of the Pope, or that of the Council? At Constance the situation was clear enough: in a series of decrees it unequivocally declared that a Council was superior to a Pope in both matters of faith and of discipline, and it required Councils to be held at frequent intervals (the decree in which it did so even begins with, and is known by, the Latin word *Frequens*). The movement which gave rise to these decisions is known as 'conciliarism'. Conciliarism was, at least in part, a reaction to the situation in which the papacy found itself (there were three rival Popes at the time), and it did not manage to survive for long. Admittedly a couple of Councils were called by reluctant Popes in accordance with the decree of the Council of Constance, including a Council which began at Basel in 1431 and which is recognised as ecumenical by the Catholic Church, but from then on the provisions of *Frequens*, which required ten-yearly gatherings, were simply ignored.

Still, the question remains, is a Council superior to the Pope? Frankly, it is not nowadays a real issue. Councils have to be convoked by the Pope of the day, and he is associated with them – he is, after all, a bishop just like the other Council fathers. All of them together have responsibility for the well-being of the whole Church – the notion of a college of bishops, discussed above in relation to the Apostolic Succession. The difference between him and the other bishops, however, is that without him a Council would not have legitimacy because he is, as we have seen (p. 21) the centre of the Church's 'communion'. In Catholic Church polity it is by being united to the Pope that bishops belong to the Catholic Church. It is certainly possible in principle that a Council might decree something which went flatly against what the Pope wished, but, as the law now stands, if the Pope did not approve such a decree it would have no binding force. It is very unlikely to happen. There have been Councils in the past which opposed a Pope's wishes, most particularly that which was called by the Emperor Theodosius II to meet at Ephesus in 449, but its binding force has never been acknowledged – indeed, its conclusions were reversed by another Council (Chalcedon) just two years later.

Councils are usually called to heal divisions rather than to create them. It has not infrequently happened, however, that some bishops have refused to accept what has been decided, and gone into schism. For instance, whole new Churches were born out of the Council of Chalcedon just mentioned because some could not accept its decision about the nature and person of Christ. More commonly, however, the Council fathers strive for consensus so that, when the final vote is taken, there is a vast majority in favour of what is being decided. It has been known for bishops to absent themselves from a Council session when they could not bring themselves to vote in favour of a decree, rather than voting against it.

At Vatican II the bishops complained that they were insufficiently involved in the running of the Church, that they were unable to exercise their collegial responsibility for the Church's well-being. It was therefore decided by Pope Paul VI that there should be regular meetings of bishops. These 'synods' meet every two years, and address issues of pressing concern, or at least those presented to it by the Pope. Not all the bishops attend: representatives are chosen from each local conference of bishops. These elected representatives constitute the majority of a synod, but the Pope himself appoints other members as he sees fit. In addition there have been special synods to deal with regions – one for Africa, for example, another for the Americas, both North and South. They commonly, but not necessarily, meet in Rome.

Such synods are obviously not distinguished from general Councils on the basis of numbers of bishops attending – more bishops go to synods than ever did to the Council of Trent. But they are not set up to be an alternative form of Council. They are not legislative bodies, like the Councils, but only advisory. This does not mean they have little or no influence. In 1971 a synod met to discuss problems about social justice. It produced a short but powerful document entitled *Justice in the World* which contained the statement 'Action on behalf of justice and participation in the transformation of the world fully appear to us as a constitutive dimension of preaching the gospel' (paragraph 6). This statement found its way into the 'canon law' of the Church, obliging priests to instruct their congregations on issues concerning social justice (cf. canon 768).

CANON LAW

The example just given of the 1971 synod is typical of what happened to canon, or Church, law. Something which had been said by a Council is turned into an instruction to be observed by the whole Church.

From the very earliest Council decrees were issued which regulated such things as the conduct of clergy. Thus in 325 the Council of Nicaea, which met primarily to discuss some heretical views, also laid down a number of rules to be observed by both the clergy and the laity – including, for instance, an instruction that at certain times of the year one was to pray standing up. There were a good many Councils, both ecumenical and provincial, which issued decrees that were sometimes thought to have had more than local significance. Also bishops, and especially the Popes, wrote letters giving instructions on what to do, or not to do, in certain circumstances. All these sources, the letters of bishops (called 'decretals' in the case of the Popes) and the decrees of Provincial and Ecumenical Councils, together constituted the law of the Church. But this mass of material, which obviously grew ever larger as time went on, was difficult to use. Letters or decrees had been issued for particular situations and might – and sometimes were – contradicted by other later letters or decrees.

This problem was tackled in the middle of the twelfth century by a lawyer called Gratian. Unfortunately we know very little about him, although he was probably a monk, and may have been an adviser to a papal judge. Disturbed by the seemingly contradictory messages coming out of the body of canon law which had been produced over the centuries, he decided to put it all into some sort of order. He compiled a book of some 4,000 different quotations of one kind or another, including some from the Second Lateran Council of 1139, and tried to reconcile them. His book is called 'The Concordance of Discordant Canons', though it is usually known as Gratian's *Decretum*. This rapidly became the text on which teachers of law lectured, and thus became something of a standard book of law for the period.

But Popes and Councils had not stopped issuing decrees. These were put into further collections which became, as it were, supplements to the *Decretum*. All these collections of laws were known collectively as 'the body of canon law' or, more commonly, by the Latin title the *Corpus Iuris Canonici*.

The *Corpus* was a rather unwieldy amalgam of texts, and at the beginning of the twentieth century it was decided to 'codify' it, a proposal which met with some resistance. Partly the resistance sprang from hostility to the memory of Napoleon, who had started the trend of codifying law in Europe. But it also sprang from antipathy to the notion of a 'code' at all: when there had been the rather disparate collection of material, drawn from different sources, there was much more room for manoeuvre and interpretation. A single code, emanating from Rome, undoubtedly did much to enhance the authority of the papacy, and abet the centralising tendency of the Vatican.

The *Code of Canon Law*, a book containing 2,414 different 'canons' or laws, was published in 1917 and came into force the following year. In the aftermath of Vatican II it was revised, and a second edition of the *Code* was published in 1983 with 1,752 canons. (A separate *Code* was produced for the Eastern rite Churches, which have different structures and discipline from the Roman Catholic Church. This was published in 1990, to come into force in 1991.)

This was law given 'from the top', rather than emanating from a variety of different sources. It inevitably gave increased prominence to the role of the Pope in the making of Church law. Not only that, the text also gave the impression that the structures of authority in the Church were in the shape of a pyramid, with the Pope at the apex. As this chapter has tried to demonstrate, the Catholic Church is, in theory, not at all like that. It is, however, the way in which many people perceive the Church, and how many people believe it to be. So next we turn to the issue of the papacy itself, and its role within the Catholic Church.

SUMMARY

1 Catholics, like all Christians, believe all authority comes from God, but it has to be exercised in this world through human institutions.
2 The transmission of this authority is called tradition.
3 Tradition, as handed on in the Church, includes Scripture as part of that tradition.
4 Scripture was produced by the Church, and the canon of Scripture was decided by the Church.
5 Oversight of the tradition is the responsibility of the Church hierarchy which stands in apostolic succession to the followers of Jesus, the apostles.

6 Serious conflicts over the interpretation of the tradition have been resolved by Church Councils.

7 The decisions of Church Councils, together with excerpts from some of the more important letters of popes and bishops, constitute the corpus of Church law, called canon law.

FURTHER READING

On Canon Law:

Coriden, *An Introduction to Canon Law*.

On authority:

McBrien, *Catholicism*, pp. 739–50.

On Scripture and tradition:

The *Catechism*, pp. 23–35.

McBrien, *Catholicism*, pp. 59–63.

O'Collins and Farrugia, *Catholicism*, chapter 3.

On models of the Church:

The *Catechism*, pp. 172–95.

Dulles, *Models of the Church*.

McBrien, *Catholicism*, chapter 19.

On councils:

The *Catechism*, pp. 204–6.

Tanner, *The Councils of the Church*.

3

PEOPLE

In the previous chapter we have looked at where authority is located within the Catholic Church. This chapter will describe the people who exercise this authority (and, at the end of this chapter, those whom the authority is exercised upon!). And there is no-one more evident in this authority structure than the Pope. In fact, perhaps nothing is more distinctive of Catholicism than the papacy. The person known as the Pope is whoever is elected to be the Bishop of Rome. Catholics certainly acknowledge the Pope as head on the Roman Catholic Church on earth. That is the easy bit. On the other hand, exactly what authority the Pope can exercise over the Church by virtue of his office is a topic hotly debated within Catholicism.

Most people outside the Catholic Church, and quite a few inside it, think that the Pope is at the apex of a pyramid. In the crudest version of this pyramidal 'model', to use Avery Dulles's term, the Pope issues orders to the cardinals, the cardinals to the bishops, the bishops to the priests, and the priests to lay people. This stark, hierarchical picture may be a fair account of how authority is exercised in, say, the armed forces, but as has already been suggested in the previous chapter, it is not quite like that in the Catholic Church. In fact, it is not at all like that, though some people – including, it seems likely, some popes in the past – have thought of it that way. Certainly the concept of the office of pope has changed down the ages, and a few paragraphs on the development of the papal office have been included in an Appendix to make that point more clear (see p. 164).

THE POPE

First of all, then, the word 'pope' itself. It comes from a Greek word 'pappas' meaning 'father'. The term is still used in Greece of parish priests, and from the third century onwards right across the Christian Church it was used of all bishops, naturally including the bishop of Rome. 'Pappas' has, however, a slightly 'familiar' feel to it, and it was only from the eighth century, when the Greek language had ceased to be used in the West, that the bishops of Rome began to use it of themselves in official documents. In the eleventh century Pope Gregory VII instructed that the term be applied to the Bishops of Rome alone, and to no one else. That more or less happened, except in Egypt where the Orthodox Patriarch of Alexandria is still known as the 'Pope'.

Catholics claim that there has been an unbroken succession of popes for the last 2,000 years, beginning with St Peter, who was appointed as head of the apostles by Jesus himself, and who came to Rome around AD 60 and was martyred there. There is good evidence in the New Testament that Peter was in some way appointed to be head of the Apostles. The text most frequently used is that from the Gospel of Matthew 16:17–18, where Christ says 'you are Peter and upon this rock I will build my Church'. The pre-eminent role Christ was assigning to Peter would have been more obvious to his immediate entourage than it is to us. It is usually presumed that Christ spoke in Aramaic, the common language of Palestine in the first century. In Aramaic the word for 'rock' is *Kepha*, and that, as a name or nickname, translates as 'Peter'. 'Peter' itself is a Greek name which comes from the Greek for rock: 'petra'.

It could, of course, be argued – and it is so argued by many – that Peter's role as leader ceased at his death, and was not passed on to any successor. But, as we have seen in the last chapter when talking about the role of tradition, early Christians certainly believed that apostolic authority was handed on, especially through some of the more important bishoprics. So, the argument runs, Peter's role among the Apostles was handed on to the bishop of Rome. Not that there is absolute proof that Peter was ever in Rome. At the Reformation and afterwards among some scholars hostile to Catholicism it was argued that Peter never journeyed to the capital of the Empire. Nowadays, however, it is almost universally agreed that he did do so – and there is abundant (though admittedly not conclusive) archaeological evidence that the basilica of St Peter's on Rome's Vatican Hill was built over the spot where Peter was believed to have been buried.

The tradition that Peter came to Rome is recorded very early. By the end of the first century two Christian writers, Clement of Rome and Ignatius of Antioch, include Peter among the Roman martyrs. He is thought to have died in the persecution of Christians by the Emperor Nero, who ruled from AD 54 to 68: Clement dates it specifically to the year 67 – and both he and Ignatius were writing within thirty years of the presumed date of Peter's martyrdom.

There is other written evidence, though of a rather later date. One piece, however, is of particular importance. Irenaeus, who became bishop of Lyons about AD 178 and died about the year 200, wrote a book entitled *Against All Heresies*. He was eager to reject the claims of some heretics who said they had 'secret' knowledge which had been handed down to them by members of their sect. Irenaeus argued that the true teachers of the faith had handed the faith on to the Christian community in an unbroken succession, and chief among these teachers, for Irenaeus, is the bishop of Rome. Irenaeus then lists the bishops of Rome to demonstrate the unbroken succession, and at the head of the list he puts Peter. Another Christian writer of the same period, the historian Hegesippus, drew up a similar list, though it only survives as it is cited in a fourth-century text. The message is clear: the true faith was handed on by the Church at Rome (and in other Churches, but we are not here concerned with these) through the succession of teachers stretching back to Peter, and this unbroken succession guarantees the authenticity of the faith that has been taught.

Is there an unbroken succession from Peter to the present Bishop of Rome, a succession that has extended over almost two millennia?

That there is such a succession is a major principle of the Catholic faith, and as I said at the beginning of the chapter, the belief in the succession is a particular characteristic of 'Roman' Catholicism. The yearbook of the central administration of the Church, the *Annuario Pontificio*, lists the popes at the beginning of the volume. According to this reckoning (and, although there are occasional complications in the course of the history as we shall see, historians do not really dispute the basic accuracy of the list), there have been 263 bishops of Rome from Peter to John Paul II. Some brief notes on the history of the papacy are given below. A longer account can be found in Appendix 1.

But it is more problematic to call St Peter 'bishop of Rome'. The first person to write about the office of bishop as the position of someone who presided in authority over his local church was Ignatius of Antioch. Ignatius – who was also the first person to talk about the 'catholic' (meaning 'worldwide') church – wrote in about the year AD 100. He, too, was martyred in Rome, sometime around 107. So if Ignatius was one of the very first bishops, then Peter, who died some forty years earlier, could not possibly have been a bishop, certainly not in the sense it is used nowadays.

THE SIGNIFICANCE OF PAPAL HISTORY

When the 'monarchical' episcopate eventually emerged in Rome, the bishops were chosen by election. We do not have any detailed accounts of the process – though we know it was frequently contested and that the election of Pope Damasus in 366 left 137 dead. The electors were, at first, the whole Christian community, but by the mid-eleventh century the right to vote was restricted to the senior clergy of Rome – the cardinals, as they were called. That is the way it has remained ever since, even though the vast majority of the cardinals who elect a pope now have only the most slender connection with the city of Rome.

It has already been remarked that the papal office is one of the most contentious aspects of Catholicism, both within and outside the Catholic Church. Many Catholics think that the office as it is now exercised has existed since earliest times. That is not so. Only gradually did the Bishop of Rome extend his authority over the whole of the Western Church. The authority of the papal office has both risen and fallen across the ages. At the beginning of the fourteenth century, for instance, Pope Boniface VIII made claims for the papacy which no modern pope would dare to make.

And the manner in which power was exercised has also changed. The way the papacy has seen its role at any point has tended not surprisingly to reflect the political structures of the day. Hence the papacy has had a feudal period, and the term 'papal monarchy' is often applied especially to the popes of the thirteenth century. Later on they became Renaissance princes, with a great deal of interest in the fortunes of their families and rather less in the good of the Church as a whole. It could even be argued that in modern times, in the 1960s and early 1970s, there has been a brief flirtation with a limited form of democracy.

For a century and a half there has been a strong centralising tendency on the part of the papacy – with the brief exception of the 'democratic' moment. There are a number of reasons for this, and they are discussed in the Appendix. There is, perhaps, no reason to suppose that centralising so much authority in the Vatican will be a permanent feature of the papacy in future generations (and possibly some reasons to suppose that it will not be), but this drift of power to the administrative centre of the Church has been given doctrinal force in what is called the 'papal magisterium', and especially in papal primacy and infallibility, two topics which formed the core of the debate at the First Vatican Council. Each of these will be discussed in turn.

THE PAPAL MAGISTERIUM

Magisterium is a difficult word. It comes from *magister*, which is Latin for 'teacher', and really defines the office of teaching, rather than what is taught, though it has long been used in the latter sense. In the middle ages the great theologian Thomas Aquinas (1225–74) distinguished between the pastoral teaching office, which was that of the bishops, and the teaching office of a master (*magister*) of theology. So all those who taught in the Church shared the magisterium in their different ways. From the early nineteenth century, however, it became increasingly restricted to the bishops; in the second half of the twentieth century it came to be used almost exclusively of the teaching office of the papacy.

There are no problems with the notion of a 'teaching office'. There might be some if the attempt were made to deny any sort of teaching office other than that of the pope and bishops. This could not be done. Great respect is shown to the teaching of very many theologians, some of them declared to be saints, down the ages. The considered opinions of the most learned and widely revered among them – such as Thomas Aquinas, for example – are regarded as a sure guide for faith and practice. This gives rise to an important distinction: some things have to be believed because they are true; some things have to be believed because of the authority of the person who says them. (One would, of course, hope and expect that the two statements amounted to the same thing.) Nowadays we have considerable hesitation about accepting something just on a person's say-so, but this has not always been the case, and certainly not in the Catholic Church. As we have seen above, there is a deep-rooted conviction that the faith is 'handed on' – the notion of tradition – which means that the Church's teaching is accepted, if not on a single individual's say-so, then on the say-so of a community of believers.

At the moment, however, we are talking of the magisterium as exercised by a single individual, whose claim to authority depends upon his office, namely the papacy. We will be looking at the most solemn form of this in greater detail in the section on infallibility. But great claims are made for what is now called 'the ordinary magisterium', a non-solemn teaching conducted by, for instance, letters sent by the popes to all the bishops of the world (encyclical letters), or by departments of the Vatican acting in the name of the pope or, in routine matters, on their own authority.

In a document published in May 1990 called 'On the ecclesial vocation of the theologian', one of the departments of the Vatican, the Congregation for the Doctrine of the Faith, wrote as follows:

> When the Magisterium, not intending to act 'definitively', teaches a doctrine to aid a better understanding of Revelation and make explicit its contents, or to recall how some teaching is in conformity with the truths of faith, or finally to guard against ideas that are incompatible with these truths, the response [of theologians] called for is that of the religious submission of will and intellect. This kind of response cannot be simply exterior or disciplinary but must be understood within the logic of faith and under the impulse of obedience to the faith.

This is a good example of the 'magisterium' being contrasted with the teaching role of theologians. It seems to suggest that, even where the teaching being proposed by the magisterium is not 'definitive', theologians – and others, presumably – are apparently expected not just to accept it but to believe it ('submission of will and intellect'). The document goes on to discuss 'dissent' from the magisterium.

There are a great many problems with this statement. There is the use of the word 'magisterium' in a very particular sense; there is the extension of the papal magisterium to a department of the Vatican; there is, it would seem, the requirement on people to believe something that may not even be true (the teaching is not 'definitive'). This cannot be the case, and in practice Catholics seem to operate what might be called a sliding scale of acceptance of teachings emanating – in particular, but not exclusively – from Rome.

THE PROBLEM OF DISSENT

There are issues where dissent is absolutely not possible for Catholics, and these will be treated below under the notion of infallibility. But such occasions are very few. There have been a number of occasions when the 'magisterium' has issued a statement which has not ultimately been accepted by the Church. This is a problematic issue, and a matter on which different parties in the Church are clearly divided, but it seems difficult to deny that even very formal statements by popes are now regarded as mistaken. The case of Pope Boniface VIII has already been mentioned (see p. 54), but there are many more examples. One has only to look, for instance, at the fulminations against freedom of conscience and of the press in Pope Gregory XVI's encyclical letter *Mirari vos* of 1832. More recently, Pope Paul VI condemned artificial means of birth control in an encyclical called *Humanae Vitae* in 1968, and this remains the Catholic Church's official teaching, repeated by subsequent popes. It is obvious, however, that very many Catholics do not accept this teaching, and practise birth control in ways not regarded as morally justifiable by the popes.

Humanae Vitae is an important example. For a century and a half or so, many Catholics had been used to accepting more or less without question what the popes had said in formal statements, such as encyclical letters. The widespread dissent from *Humanae*

Vitae challenged the authority of the pope to lay down rules and regulations. Paul VI never put his authority to the test again in quite the same way – he never wrote another encyclical, putting what from then on he wanted to say in other forms of communication. There are, of course, many Catholics who still accept papal teaching as regulating their lives, and are horrified at the degree of dissent which has been expressed. The Church therefore lives on with a clear divide in its ranks about the degree of obedience which is required to the teaching of the magisterium There is one aspect of magisterial teaching, however, which allows of no dissent, and that is infallible teaching.

PAPAL INFALLIBILITY

There is probably no more controversial, or more misunderstood, doctrine in Catholicism than the notion of papal infallibility. 'Infallibility' is defined as the inability to fall into error when teaching revealed truth. The idea of infallibility has been attached in particular to the pope, but the notion that the Church is in some sense infallible in its believing and in its teaching is widely held, even outside Catholicism. It has long been a Christian conviction that what is held and taught by all the Churches cannot be wrong. This was expressed in the 'Vincentian canon', named after Vincent of Lérins (*d. c.* 450). The 'canon' or rule is usually given in Latin. The true faith, Vincent wrote, was *'quod ubique, quod semper, quod ab omnibus creditum est'* – 'what was everywhere taught, had always been taught, and was believed by everyone'.

But then there arises the question of how we know what the faith of the Church is. It was early agreed that the bishops meeting in councils could decide on the formula which best encapsulated the Church's faith. Chief among those bishops was the bishop of Rome. His teaching was regarded as in some ways the touchstone of faith. This did not mean that the bishop, as an individual, might not fall into heresy, but if he were to do so, then he would no longer be the bishop of Rome.

The belief that the Pope was the touchstone of faith grew throughout the middle ages, but he was not formally declared to be infallible until the First Vatican Council (1869–70). The decree which declared him to be infallible is very precise in its wording.

'The Roman Pontiff', it says, 'when speaking *ex cathedra* [literally, 'from the chair'] as shepherd and teacher of all Christians, in virtue of his supreme Apostolic authority, defines a doctrine concerning faith or morals to be held by the whole Church.'

There are a number of points to notice:

> the Pope has to be speaking *ex cathedra* – in other words, very formally;
> the Pope has to be addressing all Christians;
> the Pope is *defining* something, not just making a statement;
> what he is defining is to do with faith or morals – he cannot make *infallible* statements about, for example, how the Church should be organised, or how the Church's worship ought to be performed.

The decree then goes on to say that, in those circumstances, the Pope enjoys the infallibility Christ wished for his Church with regard to faith and morals.

It also adds the much misunderstood statement that a pope's infallible utterances are 'irreformable' *of themselves*, and not with the consent of the Church. There was a school of thought (called 'Gallicanism' because of its roots in Gaul – ancient France) which held that a pope's utterances were infallible if they were accepted as such by the Church. This seems reasonable on the face of it, but it is an impossible position. The belief that lies behind papal infallibility is that the pope is enunciating a doctrine which is *already* the faith of the Church. It would be paradoxical, therefore, to allow a part of the Church to sit in judgement on it.

THE CONTEXT OF THE DECREE

It is important to remember that the decree was made in 1870, by a Council which did not have time fully to debate it. The outbreak of the Franco–Prussian war meant that Vatican I came to a rather sudden end when French troops maintaining the Pope's independence from the Kingdom of Italy were withdrawn from Rome. As a result, the question of papal infallibility, along with papal 'primacy' which was seen as closely related to it, and to which we now turn, was taken in isolation from the role of the bishops in the Church.

PAPAL PRIMACY

The opening section of this chapter discussed the New Testament and other evidence for the special authority of the pope. It was acknowledged quite early in Christian history, possibly because Rome was the capital of the Empire, though the bishops of Rome presented it as a result of their being heirs to St Peter. It was Pope Leo I (440–61) who first insisted on the Peter–Pope connection. Even before that, Church councils had acknowledged that, among the most important sees of the Church (Alexandria, Antioch, Jerusalem and, later, Constantinople), Rome came first. What this might mean in practice, however, was left unclear.

Bishops of Rome gradually extended their authority to the area around Rome, to the whole of Italy, and eventually to the whole of Europe – and, much later, beyond that. (This process is recounted in the Appendix.) Though this special authority was accepted in the Western Church, it remained undefined until Vatican I. This Council declared:

> that the primacy of the pope was intended by Christ;
> that it was the authority of a bishop over the whole Church;
> that it is 'immediate', in other words not mediated via other people (the authority is not given to the pope by, for instance, the cardinals but comes to him directly from God);
> that it is not, unlike infallibility, limited to faith and morals but covers matters of discipline and Church organisation as well.

Some Christian Churches would accept – as it seems did the early Church Councils – that the Bishop of Rome is *'primus inter pares'*, 'first among equals'. Papal primacy goes further than that, but what exactly it means has still not been clearly decided. What it does not mean is that the Pope can act in any bishop's diocese as if he were the bishop of that diocese. After the definition of papal primacy in 1870 the German Chancellor Otto von Bismarck (1815–98), who was very unsympathetic to Catholicism, claimed that bishops were being reduced to mere functionaries. The German bishops responded by saying that the definition meant nothing of the kind, and their defence of their status was approved by the Pope himself. Indeed, the definition at Vatican I expressly says that the primacy of the pope is intended only to strengthen and defend the authority of bishops.

Just as with infallibility, problems about understanding papal primacy arise in part because, as just remarked, Vatican I came to an abrupt halt. The office of the pope was treated out of the context of the office of the other bishops of the Church. Papal primacy has to be seen in relation to the Church's bishops.

BISHOPS

The word 'bishop' comes, via Anglo-Saxon, from the Greek 'episcopus' (hence episcopal and other derivatives), which occurs in the New Testament to denote the leading clergy of a Christian community: it means overseer or superintendent. It seems, however, to be used almost interchangeably with 'presbuteros' – from which we get priest (and other derivatives such as presbyterian). Presbuteros means an elder, and neither that term nor episcopus appears to involve any liturgical activity. As was remarked at the beginning of this chapter, the notion of bishop as we currently use it dates back to Ignatius of Antioch, where the title clearly implies a liturgical role both in presiding at liturgical worship and in performing baptism. Above all, the bishop is the centre of unity of his community, of the Church in his locality.

Catholics are accustomed to think of bishops as heads of their dioceses, with priests under them working in parishes, and it is to the latter that churchgoers normally relate. The bishop has become more of an administrative figure, though with some specific liturgical functions. This model had evolved by the mid-third century, together with the belief that it was the bishop who was responsible for the faith of the people in his charge. They had, in other words, the task of seeing that the faith handed down from the apostles was in turn handed on to the local community undiluted and uncorrupted. They undertook this task in collaboration with their priests and deacons (on deacons, see p. 61; there used to be a number of other offices which have now more or less died out, see box), but of course sometimes the faith they taught had to be validated by the wider Church in councils when bishops of an area, or of the wider Christian community, could meet to debate and determine matters of both faith and discipline.

BOX 3.1   OFFICES NO LONGER CURRENT

subdeacons
doorkeepers
lectors
exorcists
acolytes
lectors (readers) and acolytes (those who assist a priest during mass)
survive as 'ministries' which are, or can be, performed by lay people.
The office of exorcist (the casting out of evil spirits) can be performed
by a priest but only with permission from a bishop

CHOOSING BISHOPS

Bishops were originally chosen by the local Christian community by
a process of election, in which all sections of the community might
have their say and their vote. Over the course of time the electorate
became increasingly restricted until, in very many places, the choice
was simply in the hands of a local magnate, thus leading in the
middle ages to the conflict over 'Investiture' – see the Appendix.
However chosen, the new bishop would be ordained, or consecrated,
to the office by other bishops from the surrounding area, usually at
least three of them acting jointly. This is still the practice today,
though the process of 'election' has largely been replaced by
appointment by the pope. The pope usually makes his choice from a
list of three candidates for the episcopate submitted after consultation with, for instance, other clergy of the diocese where there is a
vacancy, other senior churchmen in a country, and possibly prominent members of the local Catholic community. The list of three
names is called a 'terna', but popes have not felt obliged to limit their
choice to these names. The process of selecting bishops is one of the
more controversial issues in modern Catholicism.

The presence of several bishops at the ordination of a new
member of the episcopate is a symbol of the new bishop's
belonging to the whole college of bishops. This is further emphasised by the requirement that all bishops in a particular area go to
Rome to discuss problems in their region with the pope and his
advisers. These visits are made every five years, and are called 'ad

limina' visits. 'Ad limina' means 'to the threshold', i.e. to the tombs of the apostles Peter and Paul, and indicates that this journey was originally seen as something of a pilgrimage.

BISHOPS AND THE POPE

As we have seen, Vatican I ended abruptly and as a consequence did not have time to consider much more than the role of the papacy. This, it is generally agreed, skewed the Church's understanding of the role of bishops in the Church. At Vatican II the office of bishop was very much at the front of people's minds. What emerged has been called the doctrine of 'collegiality'. The bishops as a college, a group, have responsibility for the whole Church, as well as having particular responsibility for their own specific part of the Church, their diocese.

They exercise this collegiality, as it is called, in various ways. There are now episcopal conferences, usually, though not necessarily, representing a nation. The collegiality is expressed most obviously in Councils of the Church, but these happen fairly rarely. More commonly collegiality takes concrete form in the synod of bishops, to be discussed in Chapter 4.

The pope, of course, is bishop of Rome. He shares in the collegial responsibility for the whole Church. He can act independently as a representative of the college of bishops, which no other individual bishop can do, and the college is not functioning as a college unless it is gathered around the pope. However, when the pope acts on his own, exercising his primacy, it is presumed that he is acting in the name of the college of bishops: he has no authority to act on his own whim, as it were, but only with the explicit, or tacit, approval of the college. The same, it should be emphasised, is true when the pope makes an infallible statement: as we have seen, he is expressing what is already the faith of the Church as taught by the college of bishops.

THE STATUS OF BISHOPS

As signs of their rank, bishops wear a ring (which in the past people used to kiss), and on formal liturgical occasions they carry a 'crosier' which may originally have been a walking stick, though it is more commonly compared to a shepherd's crook. On their heads they wear a 'mitre', a hat shaped like an inverted shield. They remain bishops to the ends of their lives, and used to continue ruling their dioceses until their deaths, though they are now expected to offer their resignation to the pope when they reach the age of 75.

A question remains whether the office of bishop is just a function, or whether it represents a different status in the Church from that of priests. Almost, though not quite all, Christian Churches which have bishops presume there is a difference in status. This is the common opinion in the Catholic Church as well, and it is endorsed by Vatican II, but there have been some theologians who believed that being a bishop was only, as it were, a particular way of being a priest.

PRIESTS

Perhaps it would be better to phrase it the other way round: priests are a limited form of being bishops. The Latin word for 'priest', *sacerdos*, was applied at first only to bishops, and the presbyters came to share in the bishop's priestly office. They acted, as it were, as delegates or representatives of the bishop in presiding at the liturgy and other liturgical functions.

The hesitation about using the word 'priest' came from the fact that the term was originally applied exclusively to Jesus. In the Old Testament priests had offered sacrifice to God; Jesus had offered the final, eternal sacrifice of himself on the cross, reconciling humankind to God. This definitive sacrifice could not be repeated, therefore there was no longer a category of priests. There remained, however, the Eucharist as a commemoration of Christ's sacrifice: at first the bishops (see p. 17 on the teaching of Ignatius of Antioch) and then the bishops' representatives came to preside over the Eucharist. Hence the presiders take on the character of priests – the relation of the Eucharist as a sacrifice to Jesus's sacrifice on the cross is one of the major issues in Catholic theology, and will be discussed on pp. 110ff.

Just as bishops were originally chosen by the Christian community they were to serve, so, too, were priests. Like the bishops they were ordained by the imposition of hands and the invocation of the Holy Spirit – there is an account of this ritual surviving in a document called *The Apostolic Tradition*, which is generally attributed to

St Hippolytus who died a martyr in Sardinia *c.* AD 236, but who had lived much, if not all, of his life in Rome. Priests could not themselves ordain, but otherwise they carried out most of the duties of bishops.

And like bishops they have to be celibate, at least in the Western part of the Church tradition (married clergy exist in some of the other rites discussed in the Introduction). The question of celibacy is hotly debated, but it seems unlikely to be relaxed in the near future, though it may be that, in places where there is a great shortage of priests, older married men may perhaps be ordained. The discipline of celibacy goes back to the early Church. It was permitted for men already married to be ordained, but marriage after ordination was forbidden (this still remains the rule in the Eastern Churches, including those in communion with Rome). And continence seems to have been expected even from those who were already married. These rules were frequently broken: many priests married, or simply lived with women (concubinage), right until the Reformation, despite the insistence on celibacy and despite the ruling of the Second Lateran Council in 1139 which declared that the marriages of priests were not only unlawful but invalid.

Within the Western Catholic Church the obligation to celibacy has remained in force. It is generally agreed that this is a matter of Church discipline, and is not required by divine law. There is a dispute about the origin of the legislation, some arguing that it stems from the ritual purity required of priests of the Old Testament, and that it is therefore inappropriate for Christian clergy. Others see it as a practical rule, to enable Catholic clergy to operate more freely than they would had they families, while others again think it reflects a tendency to assimilate the discipline of the clergy to that embraced by those who choose what is called the 'religious life' (see p. 138ff.) After an initial hesitation, the Reformers allowed their clergy to marry. There has recently been re-introduced into the Catholic Church an order of married 'deacons', alongside the deacons who are commonly on their way to priestly ordination.

DEACONS

Deacons occur in the New Testament, which mentions them as assistants to bishops. In the Acts of the Apostles (6:1–6), although the word 'deacon' is not used, seven men are chosen to serve the poor and to distribute alms. Deacons also eventually developed functions in the liturgy, but they were particularly concerned with the welfare services which Christians provided for members of their community. Deacons thus became well known, and it was very common in Rome for the bishops to be chosen from among the ranks of the deacons who, because of the services they performed, were possibly better known than the priests. The title of archdeacon was sometimes conferred on the bishop's chief assistant, even though he would usually have been a priest: this title died out in the Catholic Church, but survived in other Churches.

By the middle ages the role of deacon had diminished to minor liturgical functions, though these included reading the gospel during mass. The rank became little more than a staging post on the way to priestly ordination. But ordination to the deaconate was taken to imply a commitment to the discipline of celibacy. After the Second Vatican Council the order of deacons was enhanced by the establishment of permanent deacons, usually older men who were married – though if unmarried they were not allowed to marry after ordination. These perform a number of sacramental duties and can wear clerical dress, but in truth it is difficult to distinguish what they can do from the roles played in the life of the Church by non-ordained, 'lay' people.

THE LAITY

There has been a considerable effort in the Catholic Church over the past few decades to enhance the role of lay people who, after all, constitute the vast majority of Church members. When the Second Vatican Council began to discuss the Church it started with 'the people of God', that is to say, all Catholics, ordained or otherwise, though it then went on to talk about bishops before discussing the lay people in the Church.

The term 'laity' is derived from the Greek term 'laicos'. 'Laicos' means those who are governed, or who are subjected to taxes – and one of the chief roles of the laity has always been paying to support the clergy! But the term has a long history, almost from the beginning of Christianity (though 'laicos' does not occur in the New Testament) meaning exactly what it means today – the non-ordained, non-professional (as it were) Catholics.

In the early Church lay people had a bigger role to play than later became the norm. Not only were they consulted on important matters, but as has been seen they elected the bishops and chose the priests. These roles gradually disappeared, and the laity became almost to be defined as those who are subject to the authority of the hierarchy, though it has always been recognised that they represent the Church in the spheres of politics, business and so on which in normal circumstances the clergy are not expected to enter.

Even before Vatican II a greater role came to be envisaged for lay people, most obviously symbolised by greater participation in liturgical worship. Increasingly, however, the distinction between the lay and the clerical roles in the Church is becoming blurred, partly at least because of the declining numbers who are entering the priesthood, at least in the West. In this the Catholic Church is becoming more like the Churches of the Reform. As an English cardinal once remarked about the need for better bishops, 'The faithful need shepherds, but they don't want to be treated like sheep.' The Code of Canon Law now lays down the rights of lay people. These include the right to be engaged in apostolic activity, to study their faith (i.e., knowledge of the faith is not to be restricted by the clergy), and the right to be properly remunerated when working for the Church.

In recent years lay people have taken on a great many administrative roles, and although Church law forbids them to have 'jurisdiction', i.e. a role in governing, they are involved in decision-making from parish level upwards which is often pretty indistinguishable from governance. It is to the structures of governance we turn next.

SUMMARY

1 In this chapter we looked first at the Pope, who holds that title because he has been elected Bishop of Rome.
2 Rome played a prominent role in the history of the early Church, perhaps because it was the capital of the Empire, though the popes argued it was because the bishopric of Rome had been founded by St Peter.

3 The role of the papacy in the Church has gradually expanded and we looked at three aspects of the papacy in particular:

   a the magisterium, or teaching office;

   b papal infallibility when teaching faith or morals

   c papal primacy over the whole Church.

4 But all papal privileges are for the benefit of the Church, and are to be exercised in conjunction with the bishops.

5 Bishops rule over the local Church:

   a they are appointed by the pope, though their authority is from God;

   b they, too, were at one time elected by the local community;

   c they are assisted by priests.

6 Priests serve in parishes under the general oversight or direction of the bishop:

   a in the Western Catholic Church they are bound to celibacy.

7 Deacons are either:

   a those on the way to the priesthood; or

   b permanent deacons, who may be married;

   c both have some liturgical functions;

   d permanent deacons often have administrative functions as well.

8 Laity is the title given to the ordinary members of the Church:

   a they may not engage in governance.

FURTHER READING

On the hierarchical constitution of the Church:

The *Catechism*, pp. 203–8.

Hill, *Ministry and Authority in the Catholic Church*, pp. 1–10, 125–8.

Nichols, *That All May be One*, pp. 251–335.

On the papacy:

Hill, *Ministry and Authority in the Catholic Church*, passim.

Quinn, *The Reform of the Papacy*, passim.

     Primacy: O'Brien, *Catholicism*, pp. 751–8.

Infallibility: O'Brien, *Catholicism*, pp. 759–65.
The magisterium: O'Brien, *Catholicism*, pp. 65–6.

On the laity:

The *Catechism*, pp. 208–11.

Rademacher, *Lay Ministry*, pp. 103–222

4

STRUCTURES

The previous chapter was about people in the Catholic Church, starting with the Pope at the top of the hierarchy and working downwards, as it were, to the laity. As the Second Vatican Council insisted, however, all constitute together 'the people of God', and that status precedes any distinction of function. One of the titles that the Pope uses, after all, is 'servant of the servants of God'. The divisions of function are intended for the service of the whole Church. This chapter starts the other way round, beginning at the 'bottom' and working upwards to the Vatican and its administrative procedures at the top. It begins with the place where lay people normally gather for worship, where they primarily experience Catholicism, in the parish church.

THE PARISH

The worship of God, in whatever way worship is interpreted, is the fundamental purpose of the Church and, for that matter, of all Christians – indeed, of all, Christians or not, who believe in the existence of a creator God. One would have expected the parish, which brings people together for worship, therefore, to have ranked high in Catholic reflection and debate. It doesn't, though there is quite a range of canons (Church law) relating to the parish. The relatively small amount of discussion about the parish possibly reflects the ambiguity between a parish and the diocese to which it belongs.

In early Christianity a group of Christians was simply called 'the Church' of such-and-such a place. Such Churches were originally established in urban centres, under the charge of the bishop of the city. Gradually the bishop's jurisdiction extended outwards to include surrounding rural areas, and churches were set up in these areas to serve the local population. The whole area was known, understandably, as the bishop's 'district', for which the Latin term – derived from the Greek – was 'parochia', or parish. An alternative term, also derived from the Greek, and also used for a large administrative area of the Roman Empire, was diocese. This came into use in the fourth century, beginning in Africa. In other words, diocese and parish at first meant much the same thing: they both denoted manifestations of the local (sometimes also called the particular) Church, as distinct from the universal Church.

Nowadays, in Catholicism as in many Christian Churches, a parish is a segment of the diocese. It is defined in canon law (Canon 515 #1) as follows:

> A parish is a certain community of Christ's faithful established on a stable basis within a particular Church [i.e., the diocese in this instance], whose pastoral care, under the authority of the diocesan Bishop, is entrusted to a parish priest as its proper pastor.

The definition raises a number of issues. First of all, the parish is defined, fundamentally, as a community. Traditionally, parishes have been geographical entities. In other words, the diocese was divided up into segments, and Catholics fell, as it were, into the catchment area of a particular parish church.

This is certainly the way it used to be. The parish was the basis for many kinds of activities. Commonly there was (and often still is) a parish school, to which the parents of the parish had, and have, privileged access for their children; the priest or priests would visit the parishioners within the parish boundaries; there frequently was, and is, a hall for parish social functions. And so on. To some extent this structure still survives, but it is changing, and the quotation above recognises the change, at least in one particular: it makes no mention of parish boundaries. It does not suggest that the community is determined by a specific geographical area. There are a number of reasons for this, not least because in some parts of the world, Latin America or Africa for example, so vast are the areas served by priests that 'parish boundaries' have little meaning. And even when geographical areas are much smaller, there are in many places fewer priests, and parish visiting by the clergy has declined. This means that people feel less of a sense of belonging to a particular parish church.

There are also positive reasons why the situation has changed. Because of the way forms of worship have developed, individual churches have different ways of doing things – some are perhaps more solemn, other more casual; some have singing, others do not; and so on. Catholics increasingly tend to choose the place in which they worship according to the style of worship of a particular church. It would be wrong to exaggerate the differences, but they exist. Some churches provide particular services, for children, for different language groups, for instance, or for the disabled. Or they put on services at times which are particularly convenient, and worshippers travel there for that reason. Often in university towns the university chaplaincy is a popular place to go, possibly because people expect (though they may not always get) a better standard of preaching. There is a whole raft of reasons why people now choose one parish rather than another.

In other words, though Canon Law seems to presume that the geographical parish is the norm, there is a sense that the traditional parish structure is breaking down and the 'community' is becoming self-selecting. This could mark an important shift in the sociology of Catholicism – but that is another issue entirely.

The second feature of the definition above is that a parish is a stable entity. It has a juridical (i.e. a legal) status in Church law. However, despite the fact that a parish is primarily defined as a community, the only person who has any right to act juridically, as far as Canon Law is concerned, is the priest, a fact which rather undermines the notion of community. Indeed, the Law does not discuss the parish very much at all: most of the canons in that particular section of the Code are concerned with the duties of the parish priest. Parish councils are mentioned, but they are not obligatory, and the parish priest presides. One committee which is obligatory, however, is that which oversees finance.

All this depends on the parish priest and, above all, on the bishop, the third aspect of the definition given above. Everything depends on the bishop. He appoints or removes the parish priest. The lay people who make up the community may have a say, if the bishop so wishes, but again consultation with them depends on the bishop's own readiness to engage in such a dialogue. It is not a common happening. In practice, a parish is rarely consulted before a priest is appointed or removed, though there have been incidents where the parish community has successfully objected to a particular priest imposed on them.

BASIC CHRISTIAN COMMUNITIES

It has just been remarked that one of the challenges to the parish structure has been the shortage of priests. One imaginative response to this shortage has been the growth – especially, but not only, in Latin America – of what are known as Basic Christian Communities. They started in the early 1960s in Brazil, and are typically to be found in rural areas and in the shanty towns surrounding the cities. Though they may be visited on occasion by a priest, they are usually led by a nun or, perhaps more commonly, by a committed lay person. They meet both for worship and for social action. The members read and interpret the Scriptures in the light of their own, usually poverty-stricken, circumstances. There may be hymns and prayers, perhaps followed by a discussion of what the neighbourhood needs to do to improve the physical conditions of life. Perhaps the most famous of these communities was that of Solentiname, established by the priest-poet Ernesto Cardenal on an island in Lake Nicaragua, which attracted not only peasants but artists of all kinds.

Though the number of these communities runs to many thousand, the Catholic Church at an official level has not found it easy to come to terms with them. They are democratic, rather than hierarchical, and decisions are made by all members. All can comment equally upon the Scripture readings, though they do not have the technical knowledge which priests study to acquire. Their stance is often politically very radical, possibly to the discomfiture of the local bishop (though some bishops are very supportive). And finally they do not fit easily into the parish structure. They present an alternative way of being Catholic, though one which the Church authorities, especially those in the Vatican, view with suspicion.

DEANERIES

The Basic Communities, as has been said, lie outside the traditional structure of Catholicism. The parishes, weak though many of them are, lie firmly within it. Within the overall administrative structure of a diocese, parishes are grouped into geographical areas called deaneries. One of the local priests serves as dean, though the title itself is rarely used. In practice, deaneries nowadays have little significance in the organisation of Church life, which is dominated by the diocese, but, to give an example, deanery meetings can be used for the in-service training of clergy. This was at one time an important function, but seems now to have fallen into abeyance.

DIOCESES

As remarked above, originally the words for parish and diocese had similar meanings, and it was suggested this was the reason, in part, why so little thought had been given to parishes. On the other hand a great deal of thought has been given to dioceses – or, more correctly, to the office of bishop, the bishop being the head of a diocese. The term 'ordinary' is applied to the bishop, and he is sometimes referred to as the 'local ordinary'. That means he enjoys the 'ordinary' power of governance – whatever authority he needs, in other words, to run the diocese. (The term 'ordinary' is also applied to the Pope, because he has whatever authority he needs to do his particular job with reference to the whole Church.)

The definition of diocese in the Code of Canon Law is as follows (Canon 369):

> A diocese is a portion of the people of God, which is entrusted to a bishop to be nurtured by him, with the cooperation of the *presbyterium* [i.e. the priests – presbyters – of the diocese], in such a way that, remaining close to its pastor and gathered by him through the Gospel and the Eucharist in the Holy Spirit, it constitutes a partic-ular Church. In this Church, the one, holy, catholic and apostolic Church of Christ truly exists and functions.

Taking this definition step by step:

1   It describes a diocese as a portion of the people of God entrusted to the bishop. This suggests that the bishop himself is not a member of the people of God – but that may be splitting hairs! It also rather suggests that a bishop exists before the diocese, which is obviously not the case. Many Catholics suppose that a bishop's authority comes from the Pope. That is not the Church's teaching. A bishop's authority comes directly from God. What comes from the Pope is the assignment to a particular place.

2   There is mention of the 'presbyterium', the priests taken together as a body. This unity of priests with the bishop is symbolised in various ways: by synods, for example, which will be discussed below (cf. p. 79), but most obviously when priests and bishop celebrate the Eucharist together. They do this especially on the Thursday before Easter, Maundy Thursday as it is called, when they gather in the cathedral for the distribution of sacred oils which the bishop has blessed and which are used in certain services. The cathedral is the main church of a diocese: it takes its name from the place where the bishop has his 'seat' – which in Latin is 'cathedra'.

3   The definition goes on to call this diocese a 'particular' Church: it is the Church in that particular place. It differs from the parish, most obviously, by having a bishop rather than a priest in charge. But the really significant distinction is that the diocese is the *complete* Church. That is to say, a diocese has everything it needs for its continued existence: it is able to sustain itself. In practice, of course, that is not necessarily true: an individual diocese may not produce enough priests for its own needs. It may not have, on its own, the means of educating them, and so on. But, at least in theory it is self-sufficient.

A bishop is expected to have people to advise him. Chief among the advisers, at least in theory, is the council of priests – elected representatives of the clergy. At one time the chief advisers would have been the cathedral 'canons', priests who lived (again theoretically, because a good many of them had parishes to look after) in accommodation attached to the cathedral and provided the liturgical services of the cathedral. In the past they also looked after the diocese whenever there was a vacancy, and it was their job to provide the 'ternus' of names to the Vatican. But these tasks have been taken from them.

There is usually an array of committees and advisory bodies assisting a bishop, many of them staffed by lay people. There will commonly be a committee to look after education; there will certainly be a finance committee and one to look after buildings. There will also be a tribunal to hear marriage cases: these will be discussed below (pp. 118f.) All these make up the diocesan 'curia', or administration. In charge of the curia is the diocesan Chancellor. Another important figure is the 'Judicial vicar', or as he is commonly known, the 'officialis', who is the senior judge of the tribunal.

A bishop in a big diocese may have assistant bishops to help him. Nowadays they are often called exactly that, assistant bishops, but in the past they were known as coadjutor bishops, which means the same thing. The diocesan bishop himself chooses priests to perform that role without going through the usual process prescribed for choosing a bishop. It often happens that assistant bishops are eventually themselves given charge of dioceses.

ARCHDIOCESE

All dioceses are organised into 'provinces' – several contiguous dioceses linked together. The chief diocese of a province is usually known as an 'Archdiocese', and at its head is an Archbishop. (Some bishops are given the honorary title of Archbishop as a mark of distinction, but do not have an Archdiocese to look after.) Another title for an Archbishop is 'Metropolitan', and he has to exercise oversight of the other dioceses which are linked to his: these dioceses are called 'suffragan' sees, and their bishops 'suffragan' bishops. However, the degree of responsibility which a Metropolitan has for his suffragans is very small indeed. None the less, it is marked by a very distinctive badge of office. After a Metropolitan has been appointed he asks Rome for the 'pallium'. This is a strip of white wool which is made from the fleece of a lamb presented to the Pope on the feast of St Agnes, which is then blessed by him and put on the tomb of St Peter, in St Peter's basilica in Rome. It is worn by a Metropolitan as a sign of his authority within his province (he is not allowed to wear it outside the province), and of his communion with the see of Rome.

PRIMATIAL SEE

In many countries there is one Metropolitan see which is regarded, usually for historic reasons, as the most important. It is called the Primatial See, and the Archbishop in charge of it is called the Primate. It is a title which was originally attached to the most important city in a region, but sometimes the prominence of that particular city has been eclipsed by another one. The Primate of Spain, for instance, is the Archbishop of Toledo, though Madrid has long been Spain's capital city. It is common practice to make the Primate a Cardinal (for the title Cardinal, see below), but it is not unusual in larger countries also to make cardinals of other bishops or, more often, Archbishops.

PATRIARCHATE

The title 'Patriarch' does not mean much in the Western Church: in fact there used to be only one Patriarchate, that of the Western Church (there were several in the East), and the title of Patriarch of the Western Church still belongs to the Pope. Nowadays it is really a title of honour granted to the Archbishops of Venice and Lisbon. There is also the Latin Patriarch of Jerusalem. The title Patriarch is the equivalent of Metropolitan.

CARDINALATE

As just mentioned, senior bishops are sometimes given the title of 'Cardinal'. The term goes back to the eighth century, and it was given to the bishops of the dioceses immediately around Rome (called the subicarian sees), and to that city's senior priests and deacons. The title is thought to be derived from 'cardo', meaning hinge – that at least was the suggestion of Pope Leo IX in 1049. What distinguished the cardinal bishops, priests or deacons from other clergy in and around Rome was that they were on a rota to provide services at the major basilicas. They did this, even though they were in charge of dioceses, in the case of bishops, and of churches in Rome in the case of priests. Modern-day cardinals are still invested with the title of a Roman church or a subicarian see, so that they become, theoretically, clergy of the city of Rome. It is that which gives them the right to vote in papal elections. They are also among the Pope's chief advisers, either as heads of Vatican departments – these cardinals live in Rome – or as members of the committees which run these departments. Cardinals who do not have dioceses to look after are expected to live in Rome. Cardinals are sometimes referred to as 'Princes of the Church'.

When they really were the clergy of Rome and not just nominally so, cardinals were accustomed to act as a group, advising the Pope. At the end of the sixteenth century, when the present administrative system was set up in the Vatican, the power of the 'sacred college of cardinals' was dispersed. Individual cardinals were given particular responsibilities, so that they no longer met as a college. At least in part, this was intended to dissipate the power of the cardinals: as a group they had frequently caused popes a great deal of trouble in the middle ages. From then on they met, as a group, only on formal occasions: consistories and conclaves.

CONSISTORIES

These gatherings meet only for purely formal functions, including the canonisation of saints and the creation of new cardinals. Pope John Paul II has called the cardinals together for other reasons – to debate the finances of the Vatican, for instance. But he has made it clear that he does not consider these meetings to be consistories.

CONCLAVES

The term means 'with a key' ('con clave'), and it signifies the gathering of cardinals for the election of a new pope. The idea, which developed in the middle of the thirteenth century, was that the cardinal electors would be locked into a single room, and their lives made distinctly uncomfortable, so that they would proceed more quickly to the choice of a new pope. In fact it did not work. Papal elections still dragged on for an inordinate amount of time, and quite often cardinals died in the course of them. In modern times elections have been much swifter.

BOX 4.1   ELECTING A POPE

Only cardinals under eighty years of age may enter the conclave, but after the death of a pope all may meet, regardless of age, in 'congregations', as they are called, to continue the day-to-day business of the Church. All offices held under a pope cease at his passing, except that of the 'Camerlengo' or Chamberlain, whose job it is to run the conclave, and the 'Grand Penitentiary'.

The election begins fifteen days after a pope's death – though the period may be extended to twenty days. Hitherto the cardinals were all locked into the Vatican's Sistine Chapel and its environs. The election from now on will still take place in the Chapel, but new living quarters have been prepared for the electors in the neighbouring Hostel of St Martha. Apart from the cardinals, a few other people are allowed into the conclave area, including one personal assistant for each cardinal, called a 'conclavist'. There is a great stress on the confidentiality of the conclave, and all those attending have to take an oath of secrecy.

A two-thirds majority is needed to elect a pope (unless the number of electors is divisible by three, in which case the majority has to be two-thirds plus one). Each cardinal votes by putting a name on a ballot paper and dropping it into a chalice on the altar. When a ballot is indecisive the ballot papers are burned with wet straw, thus giving off black smoke. Without the wet straw the smoke is white – white smoke being the signal that a new pope has been both elected and accepted. The newly-elected pope chooses a name, puts on the white robes that a pope wears, and then is presented to the world from the balcony of St Peter's. Pope John Paul II has made it possible for the cardinals, if after some thirty ballots they are no nearer selecting a candidate, to move to an absolute, rather than a two-thirds, majority.

BISHOPS' CONFERENCES

A few cardinals serve the Church in full-time administration of the various departments of the Vatican, but the majority of those who have not retired are diocesan bishops. They and the other bishops of (usually though not necessarily) a particular country will meet to discuss the problems they have in common in a conference held once or twice a year. This conference generally also has a permanent secretariat, advising the bishops and carrying out policy decisions which affect the whole area covered by the conference.

BOX 4.2   ECCLESIASTICAL TITLES

These can be confusing. Priests are usually called 'Father', though in some countries this usage is restricted to members of religious orders. In Spain, for instance, the parish priest will be known as 'Don Pedro' or whatever. Bishops used to be called 'My Lord', but it is now common to call them 'Bishop'. Similarly Archbishops used to be 'Your Grace', but that has become 'Archbishop'. Cardinals, however, are still 'Your Eminence' – though the more liberal ones will be happy with 'Father'.

A good many clerics have the title 'Monsignor' before their name. 'Monsignor' is rather like a knighthood in the British honours system, and is often conferred for services to Church administration.

The different ranks can be distinguished by the style, and colour, of their official dress. But there are so many variants it would take a book in itself to explain them.

Many countries had such conferences of bishops before the Second Vatican Council; after it, however, the bishops', or episcopal, conference became part of the normal structure of the Church. Many people thought of the episcopal conference as an extension of the doctrine of 'collegiality' (the idea that all the bishops together as a 'college' are responsible for the whole Church) to the local Church of a region. The Vatican, however, has shown itself to be somewhat hostile to this idea, arguing that the bishops only act collegially when the Pope is part of the college, either personally or through his representative(s). This obviously happens in general councils of the Church, as Vatican II, but it also happens in what is called the Synod of Bishops.

THE SYNOD OF BISHOPS

This is an institution that sprang directly from Vatican II. In the course of the Council many expressed the view that the papal administration (or 'curia') was not sufficiently in touch with the bishops around the world whom, in theory, it was supposed to serve.

The Synod was the answer. It is made up of elected representatives of the episcopal conferences, special advisers, and people nominated by the Pope. It has met at irregular intervals, though roughly every two to three years, sometimes on a particular topic, occasionally to discuss problems affecting a particular part of the world.

Whether, after all, the Synod is an expression of collegiality or whether it is simply an advisory body to the Pope is a matter for debate. When originally established, it was seen as an exercise in collegiality, but in practice it has come to be advisory, with the Pope writing the document which results from the meeting. Although Vatican officials would not see it this way, turning the Synod into an advisory body represents a victory for the Vatican bureaucracy over the attempt by the bishops of the Church to influence the Church's central government.

It is to that government we must now turn.

SUMMARY

1   Parishes are the basic structural unit of the Catholic Church. They have traditionally been thought of as communities defined by geographical boundaries, but for various reasons this standard formulation has been breaking down – and in any case is hardly applicable where there is a serious shortage of priests.

2   Basic Christian Communities are a recent phenomenon, consisting of bible-reading, activist groups, especially in Latin America, which commonly operate without a priest.

3   A diocese is a geographically-defined group of parishes, under a bishop. A diocese constitutes the 'local Church' and should be self-supporting – though in practice they rarely are.

4   Bishops' conferences discuss issues, usually at a national, sometimes a regional, level.

5   The Synod of Bishops is a regular meeting of bishops from around the world (or sometimes from a particular region such as Africa, or the Americas). It is advisory to the Pope.

6   Cardinals were traditionally the Pope's regular advisers, and still perform that function from time to time when they meet in consistories. They also play a large part in managing the Vatican bureaucracy. Their best-known task, however, is electing a new Pope in a conclave.

FURTHER READING

On parishes:

The *Catechism*, pp. 468–73.

Coriden, *The Parish in Catholic Tradition*.

On Basic Christian Communities:

Hebblethwaite, *Basic is Beautiful*, pp. 52–68.

On the Synod of Bishops:

Reese, *Inside the Vatican*, pp. 42–65

Quinn, *The Reform of the Papacy*, pp. 76–116.

On cardinals:

Reese, *Inside the Vatican*, pp. 66–74

Quinn, *The Reform of the Papacy*, pp. 140–53.

On papal elections:

Reese, *Inside the Vatican*, pp. 74–105.

Walsh, *The Conclave*, pp. 159–66.

5

THE VATICAN

One of the problems when talking about the Vatican is to know exactly what is meant. There is a variety of terms which are often used interchangeably, though they have distinct meanings. First of all, the Vatican was – and is – one of the hills on which Rome was built. It was across the River Tiber from the centre of the ancient city, and outside its walls. It had a cemetery on the hillside where, Christians believed – and probably quite rightly – that St Peter had been buried. In the first half of the fourth century the Emperor Constantine built a church on the site to honour Peter. The ruins of the cemetery where Peter is thought to have been buried, and even the remains of a substantial memorial to him, probably dating from before the year AD 200, were discovered during excavations under the church during the 1940s.

Just under 200 years after the building of Constantine's church, a papal palace, the Vatican palace, was built alongside it. So, second, the Vatican was, and remains, a papal residence and, eventually, the seat of the papal 'curia' or court – the administration of the Church, tribunals, papal advisers and other officials. Catholics very often use the term 'the Vatican' to mean the papal administration, though in fact many papal offices are situated elsewhere in Rome, sometimes at some distance from the Vatican Palace itself.

Strictly speaking, this administrative entity has another, legal, name: the Holy See. It is the Holy See, for instance, which negotiates treaties on behalf of the Pope with other countries (these treaties are called `concordats', and are normally concerned with questions where Catholic practice and the law of a particular country might come into conflict – over, for example, the status of religious marriages, or the situation of Catholic education). The Holy See sends and receives ambassadors: full papal ambassadors are called papal nuncios. As this sending and receiving of ambassadors indicates, the Holy See has a recognised status as a sovereign entity in international law. International law, for instance, grants papal nuncios seniority over the ambassadors of other nations. There are other forms of papal representation for those countries where a nuncio might be inappropriate or unwelcome. Where a country does not want to receive an ambassador for whatever reason, the pope sends an Apostolic Delegate who relates not to the government but to the bishops' conference.

THE HOLY SEE

To many people, including a good many of the world's Catholic bishops, this diplomatic activity has seemed a little odd for an organisation whose authority is solely spiritual. It dates back to the time, recounted in the Appendix, when the Pope was a powerful temporal as well as spiritual sovereign, and when even the pope's spiritual authority was a powerful factor among Europe's Christian princes. During Vatican II several bishops expressed disquiet at the existence of a papal diplomatic service. They believed that they should have direct contact with the papacy, and should not have information about the situation in their dioceses mediated through papal representatives. But there is no doubt that very many countries, well over 175 at the last count, want to have diplomatic relations with the Holy See even if, as often happens, the representative in Rome also represents his or her country in some other capital city. Papal diplomats, incidentally, carry Vatican diplomatic passports, but they are drawn from priests of very many different countries who have usually attended courses in Rome for future officials of the Secretariat of State – about which, see p. 85.

BOX 5.1   'SEE'

The word 'See' is equivalent to 'diocese'. It comes from the Latin for 'seat' (*sedes*), and indicates the area over which a bishop has responsibility.

There is another Latin word for 'seat', *cathedra*. It is used of the formal chair on which a bishop sits during functions in his own church. His own church is the place of the *cathedra*, and therefore is called a cathedral.

THE VATICAN CITY STATE

Third, the term Vatican might mean the Vatican City State. This came into existence in 1929 by a series of agreements with the (then) Kingdom of Italy in order to guarantee the papacy a degree of independence. The Vatican City State is in extent by far the smallest country in the world, with the fewest number of inhabitants. It includes the area immediately around St Peter's, some 'extraterritorial' buildings in various places around the city of Rome, and the papal Summer residence at Castel Gandolfo just outside Rome. Many people think that it is as sovereign of the Vatican City State that the Pope sends and receives ambassadors, but this is not so. He does so in his capacity as head of the Holy See, the administrative body of the Catholic Church.

THE CURIA

There are situations where it may be necessary to keep the above distinctions in mind, but generally speaking when Catholics refer to the Church's administrative body they call it 'the Vatican' (or, sometimes, 'Rome' or 'the Curia'), and when they say 'the Vatican' it is often shorthand for a group of administrative departments, the Roman term for which is 'dicasteries'. 'Dicastery' is a useful word (it comes from the Latin meaning 'ministry'), because it covers different types of administrative machinery, some of which will be described in the following sections. The 'dicasteries' covered here are the more important ones. As with any government bureaucracy, their shape and form – and the number of them – has changed over time to meet new needs. A good many popes have drawn up new structures for their curia, the origins of which must come from the earliest years of the papacy though very little is known until the literary figures such as Pascal and Voltaire, and popular novelists like Dumas, both father and son. Even scholars who needed to use these forbidden volumes were expected to ask permission to read them. This repressive regime has disappeared. It is not uncommon for authors to seek ecclesiastical approval for a work by submitting it to the local bishop. He in turn will then issue an 'imprimatur', which literally means 'let it be printed', and this permission is sometimes given prominence. But no one nowadays would attempt to forbid Catholics from reading anything, even books which the CDF had declared to be heretical.

CONGREGATION FOR THE EVANGELISATION OF PEOPLES

If the Secretariat of States looks after the general administration of the Church and the CDF the purity of faith within the Church, the task of the Congregation for the Evangelisation of Peoples [or Nations] is to extend the reach of the Church. It is, in other words, in charge of the Catholic Church's missionary activity. When it was founded, at the very end of the sixteenth century, it was known by its Latin title '*De propraganda fide*' – literally, 'for spreading the faith' – and was commonly called simply 'Propaganda'. But that term has now very unhappy connotations (even the *Oxford English Dictionary* gives 'the Congregation of Propaganda' as the origins of the term 'propaganda'), and it was renamed in 1967. This Congregation has charge not just of spreading the Catholic faith, but of administering those regions of the world where the standard structures of bishops and dioceses have not been fully established. In practice this amounts to vast areas – practically the whole of Africa and Asia, and parts of Latin America, among others. It supervises clergy who work in those parts of the world, and likewise all the nuns or other pastoral workers involved in schools, health centres and so on. It also trains missionaries – there is a special University in Rome, the Urbanianum, founded in 1627 and taking its name from the Pope, Urban VIII, who created it.

The Congregation has a wide range of activities, from gathering detailed statistics on missionary activity to publishing magazines in numerous of languages. Because it has had such a long history – in its present form it dates from 1622 – it has a particularly important archive which contains reports back to the Congregation from

late fourth century. However, the form in which the curia exists today really dates from the pontificate of Pope Sixtus V who, in his bull *Immensa dei* of 1588, divided up the papal administration into fifteen departments, called Congregations (or, more correctly, 'Sacred' Congregations, though the term sacred will not be used here to avoid repetition), most of which had, and still have, a cardinal at their head, usually known as the Cardinal Prefect.

SECRETARIAT OF STATE

In the government of the USA, the Secretary of State is the person in charge of foreign relations. This has led to some confusion about the role of Secretary of State in the Vatican. The Cardinal Secretary of State, a title which dates back to the middle of the seventeenth century, is in effect the papal Prime Minister, ultimately responsible for both the issues arising internally within the Church, and those relating to other states. There are therefore two major departments: General (formerly called 'Ordinary') Affairs of the Church, and Diplomatic (formerly called 'Extraordinary') Affairs. Each of these two departments is under the charge of a Vatican official who is commonly known by the Italian title 'Sostituto'. 'Sostituto' is, as one might expect, the Italian for 'substitute' – but it also means 'deputy': the heads of these two sections of the Secretariat are therefore run by Deputy Secretaries of State, who have the rank of Archbishop.

The section entitled General Affairs deals with all communications to the Holy See, and therefore has within it officials who specialise in the main modern languages – but also in Latin, which is still the official language of major Vatican documents. Its departments include subsections which deal with all the usual things one might expect, including ceremonial and protocol and the encrypting of documents going to papal diplomatic representatives. It is also responsible for overseeing the whole of the papal curia, and dealing with promotions within it. The Department for Relations with States has oversight of the papal diplomatic services themselves, and of its representation on international organisations: the Holy See has 'observer status' at the United Nations, for example. The Holy see may not, according to the terms of the agreement it drew up with Italy in 1929, become involved in any conference or negotiation where its neutrality may be put at risk – thus the 'observer status' rather than full membership. It is, however, a full member of some of the UN's agencies such as the High Commission for Refugees and the Conference on Trade and Development. The Department for Relations with States is also concerned with 'concordats', or treaties, between the Holy See and other states, and in general what might be called the Holy See's 'foreign policy'. During the latter period of the Communist domination of Eastern Europe, for example, the Secretariat was engaged in delicate negotiations to improve the conditions for Catholics in several of the countries of the Soviet bloc, and to obtain the release of imprisoned clerics. A more recent high-profile problem has been the relations between the Holy See and the State of Israel, which until recently the Holy See refused to recognise because it wants to see Jerusalem as an open city, rather than, as Israel insists, the capital of that country.

CONGREGATION FOR THE DOCTRINE OF THE FAITH

Whereas the Secretariat of State is concerned with the nuts and bolts of papal administration, the Congregation for the Doctrine of the Faith – often abbreviated by Catholics to the initials CDF – is, as its title indicates, concerned with what is central to most if not to all religious faiths, namely, the question of what is to be believed by the faith's adherents. It is often described as 'the Vatican's doctrinal watchdog'. So important is it that it used to have, until 1965, the title 'Supreme Congregation', and the Pope himself, rather than a Cardinal, was its Prefect: the Cardinal who handled the day-to-day business was therefore known as the Secretary. It was in this respect brought into line with the other Congregations in 1967.

The CDF is the oldest of the Congregations, founded in the middle of the sixteenth century as the Roman Inquisition, its name being changed in 1908 to the Holy Office. It assumed its present name in 1967. Its role is to promote and protect the faith, though the latter activity is rather more obvious, and a good deal more controversial, than the former. From time to time it issues documents about doctrinal matters, which is the 'promotional' element, but it is more often seen as, or perhaps more commonly understood to be, condemning the writings of the more controversial theologians.

BOX 5.2   THE INQUISITION

The Inquisition was formally established in 1231 to combat a pa[...] heresy in what is now France. There was not one Inquisition but [...] the lurid stories mostly relate to the Spanish Inquisition. Recent re[...] indicates, however, that the number of people who were execu[...] deviating from Catholicism was only a tiny proportion of those a[...] charged with heresy. Executions – and torture – did indeed h[...] though far more often in Spain than in Rome. In Spain there [...] concern about national unity, which was linked to a national unity i[...] – this was long before the notion was accepted that several re[...] might exist peacefully side by side.

This procedure used to be very secret: the author [...] condemned for his or her views would not be told (and still [...] told) who the accuser has been, but now at least such theol[...] have the possibility of defending themselves. Catholic bishop[...] in the past expressed disquiet about the way the CDF op[...] accusing it of not operating justly. This is quite apart from th[...] that, certainly in the eyes of many Catholics, the CDF stifles [...] about theological issues which are in theory at least open to d[...] sion. It has on the whole taken, perhaps understandab[...] conservative stance on doctrinal matters. In the 1980s, for exa[...] the radical 'theology of liberation' which was widespread a[...] Catholic theologians in Central and South America drew its [...] and it has effectively silenced a number of distinguished theolo[...] scholars, at least for a time. Some of them have subsequently [...] the priesthood so as to be able to write freely.

Indeed, one of the best-known responsibilities of the predeces[...] of the CDF, the Roman Inquisition, was the drawing up of the *I*[...] *of Forbidden Books*. The Roman version of the 'Index', as it [...] commonly known, lasted from the middle of the sixteenth cent[...] until the middle of the twentieth – it was abolished in 1966. [...] Index was a book, revised at regular intervals, which listed the w[...] ings of novelists, philosophers, theologians and others, wh[...] Catholics were prohibited from reading because, it was thought,[...] read them would be detrimental to the reader's faith or morals. T[...] banned writers included philosophers as important as David Hum[...]

missionaries down the centuries. Because missionaries were very often the first Europeans to stay long in some of the more remote places of Africa and Asia, the archive is a particularly valuable source of information on the history of these areas.

THE CONGREGATION FOR BISHOPS

The Congregation for Bishops is in some ways the Church's 'home civil service'. It has the responsibility of looking after the structures of the Church in all those countries which fall outside the remit of either the Congregation for the Evangelisation of Peoples, or the Congregation for the Eastern Churches mentioned in the next section. When new dioceses have to be established, or old ones suppressed or amalgamated, this falls to the Congregation of Bishops. Its main work, however, is organising the appointment of bishops to vacant dioceses, gathering the information, and making recommendations to the Pope who, in the present way of running the Church (it must be stressed that it was not always thus), has the job of formally choosing bishops in all but a tiny number of instances. It has already been remarked that the selection of bishops was one of the more controversial aspects of Catholic life, at least in recent times. And the Congregation for Bishops is the reason. The ideal is that bishops should be chosen from among the clergy of a diocese, and that all members of a diocese should have a say. The obvious way of achieving this is by a straightforward election process by all members of the Christian community. This we know was the method used in the early Church – though it was in practice anything but straightforward. Because the nobility gradually began to control episcopal appointments in their territories, in the middle ages Rome tried to wrest the appointment from the control of lay people and retain it for itself. In the event a number of different forms of 'election' emerged, but the canons of cathedrals came to play a significant role, submitting names to Rome. There were customarily three names, the 'terna' as it was called, with the preferred person named first. In some – a very few – instances this is still the case, with the Pope, at least in theory, doing no more than confirming the decision of the canons. That, however, is not now the common way of doing things.

The local Church still has some say in the choice. Every three years the local bishops' conference is supposed to meet in secret to draw up a list of possible candidates for the office of bishop, and this list is forwarded to Rome. However, when there is a vacancy the papal representative in a country, either a nuncio or an apostolic delegate (see p. 83), takes a hand. He is required to consult the bishops of the region, the advisers to the diocese where the vacancy has occurred, and the canons of the cathedral – or at least some of them. He may also consult more widely among priests and laity. But all this is to be done in secret. He then sends the traditional three names to Rome, where the list is vetted by the Congregation for Bishops, and a choice (which indeed need not be one of the priests recommended) is made. The process is controversial because it give the Vatican complete control over the selection of bishops. The Congregation, it is believed, chooses candidates in line with papal policy rather than those best suited to the needs of a particular diocese. It is also thought to have a tendency to choose priests who have received much of their ecclesiastical training in Rome in preference to priests trained in their home country. Defenders of this system point out that it is a great benefit for a bishop to have had some first-hand experience of the Roman system, and they also point out – with some reason – that leaving the choice of a bishop to the local community can lead to 'inbreeding', a lack of innovation and, in the worst case, corruption.

There is one further responsibility of the Congregation of Bishops: it is charged with arranging the *ad limina* visits of bishops to Rome. *Ad limina* means literally 'to the thresholds', and the thresholds in question are those of the tombs of the Apostles Peter and Paul. They are, in other words, occasions when bishops from round the world come in turn to make a report on their dioceses. This practice, which dates back to the middle ages, is required of European bishops every five years, and of those from further away every decade or so. Nowadays they are usually arranged for a whole episcopal conference at a time, unless it is too large a group. A visit to the Congregation for Bishops is part of these *ad limina* visits. Normally also there is an audience with the Pope. To show that they have indeed made a visit to 'the thresholds of the Apostles', bishops are required to sign registers in the basilicas of St Peter's and St Paul's to demonstrate that they have been there.

OTHER CONGREGATIONS

As should be evident from what has already been said, there have been a number of different Congregations responsible for particular aspects of the Church's life. Some have disappeared, others merged, and there have been a good number of name changes since the sixteenth century, when the present structure came into being. The Church's liturgy, for instance, its form of worship which will be discussed in the next chapter, is overseen by the Congregation for Divine Worship. Falling under the remit of this Congregation are topics such as the manner in which the liturgy is celebrated, the translation into the many languages used in worship from the (usually) Latin original text, and the times and occasions of particular celebrations – in other words, the liturgical calendar. The calendar lists the days on which the lives of saints are to be commemorated, which is normally, though not always, the day they died (this day is regarded as their 'birthday' into heaven). It also indicates how significant a feast any individual celebration is, an important consideration because quite frequently two feasts will occur on the same day. The Congregation responsible for creating saints to be listed in the calendar and to be venerated by Catholics is the Congregation for the Causes of Saints. The workings of this dicastery will be discussed later (see pp. 131ff.)

It was pointed out at the beginning of this book that the term 'Roman Catholic' can be misleading. There are Churches in communion with Rome which are not 'Roman' in their way of doing things. In particular they have never had a liturgy which is, or was, celebrated in Latin. These are the Eastern or Oriental Churches, which have their own ecclesiastical discipline, structure and way of carrying out the liturgy. They are looked after by the Congregation for Eastern Churches. This carries out the responsibilities, summarised in the paragraphs above, of the Congregations for Bishops, and it has oversight as well of ecumenical relations with the Orthodox Churches (those with similar rites to the Eastern Churches, but not in communion with Rome). The geographical region over which this Congregation exercises authority extends from Albania down through Greece and the Middle East to Afghanistan, and includes Egypt and part of Ethiopia. Obviously Catholics in these areas come into regular contact with Muslims, and the Congregation is also active in fostering relations with Islam. Of course, many Catholics who belong to Eastern Churches do not live within these geographical limits but, for one reason or another – Communist persecution during the Cold War, for instance in countries such as Armenia and the Ukraine, or problems with Israel for the Palestinian Christians – have emigrated to the West. These émigrés, wherever they are to be found, are also the responsibility of the Congregation for Eastern Churches.

The Congregation for the Clergy has oversight of the formation and training of diocesan priests, except in areas under the Congregations for the Evangelisation of Peoples and for the Eastern Churches. It also is concerned with the management of diocesan property.

The Congregation for Institutes of Consecrated Life and Societies for Apostolic Life – a rather long-winded title which was adopted only in 1988 – has similar concerns to those of the Congregation for the Clergy in matters to do with religious orders and other special states of life within Catholicism. These will be discussed later (see pp. 138ff.)

Finally among the Congregations is that for Catholic Education. When it was established it had responsibility for overseeing education in Rome, and eventually throughout the papal states. Its chief concerns nowadays, however, are threefold. First, it oversees seminaries for the training of clergy. It therefore has a concern for the curriculum and for the standards required in priestly formation. Second, it has responsibility for Catholic colleges and universities throughout the world, of which there are some 600. Its ability to intervene in the affairs of these varies from institution to institution: a very few are 'pontifical' faculties, which are closely controlled; in others the Congregation's remit is limited to the teaching of religion. It has demanded in recent years that those teaching theology in professedly Catholic colleges have explicit approval (called a *missio canonica*) from the local bishop. It would be fair to say that this requirement has not been implemented everywhere with the same success. Third, the Congregation has oversight of all Catholic education at primary and secondary level – which means oversight of 150,000 schools with, in all, about 40 million pupils. With so large a remit, the degree of oversight, though again it varies from place to place, is relatively small. It is unlikely that pupils and their parents – or even many of the staff of such institutions – are aware of the Congregation.

PONTIFICAL COUNCILS

When he became Pope in 1958, John XXIII decided to call a council of all the bishops of the Catholic Church – the Second Vatican Council, which has been mentioned several times. It seems likely that, at least at first, one of the purposes of this Council was to work towards a restoration of unity between Catholics and other Christian Churches. To that end Pope John set up a Secretariat for the Unity of Christians – later to be renamed the Secretariat for Promoting Christian Unity. He put at its head an eminent Scripture scholar, Cardinal Augustine Bea. Its brief was to establish links with non-Roman Catholic Christians in order to improve relations and foster the restoration of unity.

It was significant that this new body was not called, or put under the supervision of, a Congregation. There was an obvious attempt by Pope John to set up new ways of doing things, a 'new curia' in other words, which was not as governed by the same traditions as the other, long-established, dicasteries. In the preparation for the Council it became clear that the new Secretariat was much more open than some of the older institutions of the Roman Curia when Cardinal Bea clashed with the head of the Holy Office (the Congregation for the Doctrine of the Faith as it is now known) over religious toleration. It was the position adopted by the Secretariat, rather than that championed by the Holy Office, which was finally accepted in the course of the Council.

The success of the Secretariat led to its becoming a permanent body within the Roman Curia in 1966. In 1988 it was renamed a Pontifical Council. This last development also applied to the other Secretariats which had been set up. They were that for Non-Christians, created in 1964, and for Non-Believers, created the following year. The names were found to be, in a sense, too pejorative – the expected dialogue partners being defined by what they were not rather than by what they were. So the titles were changed to Council for Inter-Religious Dialogue and Council for Culture, respectively. Strictly speaking, the Secretariat for Non-Believers was absorbed into an already existing Council, for the task was too amorphous. The dialogue partners who were envisaged included Marxists, humanists, atheists and so on. But members of the Secretariat found that there was no representative body of any of these groups with whom they might open discussions. To some extent, it has to be said, the same has proved to be true of the Council for Inter-Religious Dialogue: there is no one body which represents all Muslims, for instance, nor one which represents all Jews, still less all Hindus or Buddhists. There are a number of other Pontifical Councils of varying importance. The Council for Justice and Peace was first set up in 1967 to promote understanding of the Church's teaching on social issues. 'Cor Unum' ('One Heart') coordinates the Catholic Church's main charitable organisations, such as Catholic Relief Services (CRS) in the USA or the Catholic Fund for Overseas Development (CAFOD) in England and Wales, working in the area of emergency relief and overseas development. It is itself also a charitable organisation, working with dioceses throughout the world to aid the poor and underprivileged. In addition to these there are Pontifical Councils for Migrants, for Health Workers, for the Family, and for Social Communication, which is what the Vatican calls the mass media. Finally in this category is the Pontifical Council for the Interpretation of Legislative Texts. When the first Code of Canon Law was promulgated in 1917 a commission was established to rule on how the Code was to be interpreted. This commission became a Pontifical Council in 1988. Its task still remains to adjudicate on the interpretation of Canon Law, including that of the Eastern Churches. It also advises on the Code when need be, and is charged with ensuring that any local legislation agreed by bishops of a particular country is in conformity with the law of the whole Church.

VATICAN FINANCES

The Vatican is, as has already been said, a small state, and it has all, or most, of the offices which go to make up a state. There is, for instance, a tiny army, the Swiss Guard. Originally these were a group of mercenary soldiers, recruited in the first instance in 1506. The Guard, drawn from the Catholic cantons (departments or provinces) of Switzerland, has for the most part been in existence ever since. It is a force of some 100 men and has responsibility for the security of the Pope, though, in its picturesque uniform which dates from 1914–15, it is more commonly seen on ceremonial duty. Then there is what might be called a national library, the Vatican Library (or, more correctly, *Bibliotheca Apostolica Vaticana*), whose collection of books, and especially of manuscripts, in its present form dates from the fifteenth century. It is an extremely important collection, and much used by scholars. So, too, are the Archives, which contain records for the papacy from the beginning of the thirteenth century onwards, though there is some earlier material. These papal documents often travelled around with the papacy, and in 1810 a great deal of material was, on the orders of Napoleon, transported to France: more left Rome than arrived in Paris. The papers were returned in 1817, though not all of them found their way back. The Archives are called 'the Secret Archives', which makes them sound somewhat sinister, but in this context 'secret' simply means 'private'. They have been available to scholars since the end of the nineteenth century, though (as in any archive) there is a time limit to what may be consulted. In the pontificate of John Paul II that time limit was significantly reduced. Scholars can now consult them from six popes back. Again like a any state, there is a radio station, Vatican Radio, which began operations in 1931. It broadcasts in many different languages information, about the papacy and about the Church in general, as well as carrying religious services. There is even a Vatican television service, though this is a much smaller operation, producing programmes about the pope and distributing them.

Finally in this catalogue, mention must be made of the Vatican Railway, a very short stretch of line with a particularly splendid station at the end of it, linked to the Italian rail network. It has rarely carried passengers. Most traffic consists of goods entering the Vatican City State. The Vatican City State has even claimed the right to establish its own airport and airline – but it does not have one. In fact airspace above the Vatican is banned to all flights.

All these enterprises cost money. Until the disappearance of the papal states in the mid-nineteenth century (see pp. 58, 174) there was an income from taxes and property. There was also a 'tax', started by King Offa in England towards the end of the eighth century, and paid by the English fairly regularly from the end of the eleventh century until the Reformation. When the papal states were lost to the papacy, the English renewed their contribution: it was now called 'Peter's Pence'. The idea spread to other European countries and to the United States. This was, and remains, a regular source of income, though as it depends on the generosity of the Catholic faithful the amount sent to Rome varies year to year.

In 1929, when the Vatican City State was created, the Italian government handed over 750 million lire in recompense for the loss of the papal states. The complete deal was rather more complicated than that, but basically this sum provided the funds on which the Vatican was able to operate. A committee, simply called 'the special administration', was set up to look after the money. In addition, from 1887 there had existed the 'Istituto per le opere di religione' (IOR) – the 'Institute for the works of religion' – which had been established not directly to handle the Vatican's own money, but donations of whatever form which had been made to religious orders. In 1942 the IOR, or 'the Vatican bank' as it is popularly though incorrectly known, was also given the task of managing Peter's Pence. In 1984, the IOR's involvement in the scandal of the collapse of Milan's Banco Ambrosiano cost it nearly $241 million. The IOR survived, but its governance was tightened up, a board of five lay Catholic bankers being appointed to supervise it. The IOR remains basically an investment bank, but it has current accounts for the religious orders for which it was first established, and for the Vatican itself and for some Vatican employees.

This is far from the whole story. For instance, the Vatican makes money on the goods it imports and sells to its employees and some others from within the Vatican City State. It also, and famously, makes money out of its stamps and, to a lesser extent, its coins (it uses the same currency as Italy). Moreover some dicasteries, especially the Congregation for the Evangelisation of Peoples, have their own income separate from that of the Vatican itself. The Vatican now produces annual accounts. It almost always runs at a loss.

SUMMARY

This chapter has been concerned with the central administration of the Catholic Church.

1　The central administration is commonly referred to as 'The Vatican', but this term has several meanings for Catholics:

    a   it is a hill, on which the basilica of St Peter's was built in the fourth century;

    b   it is a palace, now lived in by the popes;

    c   it is the central administration itself, otherwise known as 'the Curia' (the 'court');

    d   it is an independent city-state, created in 1929;

    e   under the title 'the Holy See' it is a legal, sovereign body in international law.

2 The Curia is divided up into departments, some called Congregations, others Pontifical Councils, or a variety of other names. The main departments are:

    a   The Secretariat of State, concerned both with the internal organisation of the Church and its relations with other states;

    b   The Congregation for the Doctrine of the Faith, concerned with doctrinal orthodoxy;

    c   The Congregation for the Evangelisation of Peoples, responsible for the Church's missionary activity;

    d   The Congregation for Bishops, which oversees the appointment of bishops and organises their regular *ad limina* visits to Rome;

    e   Other Congregations have responsibility for worship, for the creation of saints, for the well-being of the Eastern Churches in communion with Rome and so on;

    f   Pontifical Councils were created in the last half century, and include departments with responsibility for improving relations with other Christian Churches, or with other faiths, such as Islam, or for promoting justice and peace in the world.

3 All this requires money: the Vatican receives this from a variety of sources, including:

    a   the settlement after the 1929 Lateran Treaty establishing the Vatican City State;

    b   Peter's Pence.

4 The Vatican Bank (*Istituto per le opere di religione*) administers some, though not all, of the Vatican's finances.

FURTHER READING

On the legal position of the Holy See:

Cardinale, *The Holy See and the International Order*, pp. 73–97.

On the legal position of the Vatican City State:

Cardinale, *The Holy See and the International Order*, pp. 99–128.

Reese, *Inside the Vatican*, pp. 16–24.

On the organisation of the Vatican:

Pollard, *Money and the Rise of the Modern Papacy*, passim.

Quinn, *The Reform of the Papacy*, passim.

Reese, *Inside the Vatican*, pp. 106–39.

THE LITURGY

The main religious purpose of all Christians is the worship of – in other words, showing honour and reverence to – God. Worship in this sense is not specifically Christian. It is to be found in all religions. The form it takes naturally varies from religion to religion, but within Christianity most Churches have rather similar forms of public worship. This public worship is called 'the liturgy', and it comes from two Greek words meaning 'public' and 'work'. The 'liturgy', then, is something done in public, and is a corporate act – that is to say, it is (usually) not done by individuals on their own. One has to use the word 'usually' here because in many Churches, certainly the Anglican and Catholic Churches, the liturgy is in a sense prescribed, and some think it should take place whether or not there is anyone present – apart, obviously, from the person carrying out, or presiding at, the liturgy, who is known as 'the celebrant'.

As well as these public rituals, or rites, there are also private ones. Some of these private ones, which are very common in Catholicism, will be described in the next chapter. They are less common outside Catholicism: the Reformation did away with many of them, though some have again been growing in popularity in non-Catholic Churches over the last couple of centuries.

CATHOLIC WORSHIP

The public liturgy, partly precisely because it is public, is very structured in Catholicism. As will be seen, there is no doubt that it started as a fairly simple ritual, but down the ages it became increasingly elaborate – except for those periods, or places, when there was an effort within Catholicism to return to a simpler form. There was one such reform of the complex ritual of the main Catholic act of worship, the mass, in the second half of the twentieth century. The most obvious sign of this was the abandonment of the use of Latin in the liturgy, and its replacement by the vernacular language of each local Church.

This translation of the liturgy into modern form had happened four hundred years earlier for non-Catholic Churches. The range of forms of worship in them became over the centuries very diverse. Largely through the influence of the Vatican, Catholicism for the most part managed to maintain a more or less standard form of public worship. In more recent times, however, there has been a gradual growing together of the styles of worship of at least some of the Churches, including the Catholic Church.

These changes have not always been well received by Catholics. The translation of the liturgy into the vernacular was much regretted by some, who believed that the air of mystery which should surround the Church's main act of worship had largely disappeared. Latin was not banned when the liturgy was translated, but in practice it has been little used. There were others who felt that the changes had not gone far enough, that the Vatican had effectively stopped the liturgy being adapted to the needs of different parts of the world. One particularly controversial issue, for example, was the use of inclusive language (i.e., not using 'man' or 'he' when people of both genders are intended), both in the liturgy itself, and in the translation of those passages of Scripture which are read out during the liturgy. There was an even more radical criticism of the changes. There were those who believed that the form of the mass which had been established at the end of the sixteenth century (called 'the Tridentine' missal after the Council of Trent) was in some sense 'true', and that the new form, often referred to as 'the missal of Paul VI', was somehow heretical. People who held this view tenaciously ended up outside the Catholic Church.

The word 'mass' has just been used. It needs a little explanation. This word is the one most commonly used for the central act of worship of the Catholic Church. A better term would be 'the Eucharist', which is becoming more widely used. The word 'mass' is an odd one. It seems to come from the Latin 'missio' or 'sending'. In the Latin form, the mass ends with the words *'Ite, missa est'*, a phrase which is usually translated as 'Go, the mass is ended', but perhaps ought to be translated as 'Go, it is the sending [out]'. It is from 'missa' that the word 'missal' comes – the missal is the book which contains the texts for the mass. It came into existence in the tenth century. Before then there were a number of different books containing different parts of the mass.

The missal also contains the 'rubrics', the regulations governing the way the liturgy is to be carried out. These are laid down by the Congregation for Divine Worship (see p. 91). They are called 'rubrics' because, in the middle ages, they were written in red so that the celebrant could distinguish the ceremonial instructions from the text of the ceremony itself. And the missal also contains the Church's liturgical calendar.

THE CALENDAR

The liturgical calendar is the way in which the various important occasions in the Church's year are arranged on an annual basis. These include commemorations of the Church's saints, but more important are the commemorations – or 'feast days' – which recall the life of Christ. There is an important point here. Christianity claims to be an historical religion. That is to say, it arises from the life, death and resurrection from the dead of Jesus Christ, and these events happened in recorded time. They are not myths or stories but real happenings, even if the recording of these stories has sometimes been wrapped up in a form of almost mythological language. Because these important events happened in a particular period of time, it is possible to commemorate them, and to commemorate them in a cycle of feast days which recalls – in a way recapitulates – the life of Christ. So, in the course of a year, the Christian worshipper (there is nothing specifically Catholic about the general principle) remembers the life of Jesus in a kind of chronological order.

What is more problematic, however, is the issue of what date to assign to which feast. The easiest way to begin is to start with Easter, the day of Christ's resurrection. In the accounts of Jesus's life, the crucifixion is associated with the Jewish feast of Passover. (In most European languages other than English, this link is reflected in the name of the season; in English it is apparently derived from the name of the Spring goddess of the Anglo-Saxons.) This meant that Christ's resurrection took place on the day we now call Sunday. The Passover falls on the Jewish calendar date of 14–15 Nisan, but the Jewish calendar being lunar does not often coincide with the one Christians now use. This led to disputes in early Christianity about which date to use, some wishing to keep to the Jewish date for Passover whereas others (those in Rome for instance) preferring always to celebrate Easter on a Sunday. There were a great many controversies about the date of Easter, and although Christians now generally agree on a date, the Orthodox Churches generally have a slightly later one. The formula for deciding what day is Easter is that it falls on the Sunday following the first full moon after the Spring equinox. This means that it can fall on dates which are a month apart, the earliest being 21 March, the latest 25 April.

The date of Easter affects a number of other dates in the calendar. According to the New Testament, Jesus rose into heaven forty days after the resurrection: so the Feast of the Ascension is forty days after Easter – always a Thursday. Then fifty days after Easter the Holy Spirit came down upon Jesus's followers: the feast of Pentecost (a Sunday). Easter was preceded by a period of preparation, which in English we call Lent (from the Middle English for Spring), but which again in most European languages is derived from *Quadragesima*, meaning forty. The period of forty days, or six weeks, begins with Ash Wednesday, when Catholics are marked on their forehead with ashes. The Sunday before Easter is commonly called Palm Sunday, marking the entry of Christ into Jerusalem, when he was greeted by the people of the city waving palm branches. This begins a particularly solemn time, Holy Week, the last three days of which are the 'Sacred Triduum' of Maundy Thursday, commemorating the Last Supper, Good Friday, commemorating the crucifixion, and Holy Saturday, when nothing happens – to mark Jesus being in the tomb. 'Maundy', incidentally, comes from '*mandatum*' or command –

Jesus's command to 'love one another as I have loved you', which is symbolised in the Maundy Thursday service when the celebrant washes the feet of some of the congregation.

These, then, are the main 'moveable' feasts of the Christian calendar. Most, however, are fixed to a particular day in the year. The best-known, of course, is Christmas, the feast of the birth (the 'nativity') of Jesus. It is generally said that the feast of Christmas was fixed on 25 December because this had been a pagan festival. There is another possible explanation. It was thought by some in the early Church that Jesus was conceived, and died, on the same day of the year, and as they thought Jesus died on 25 March then he must have been conceived on 25 March. This is the feast of the annunciation when, according to the Gospel, an angel announced to Mary that she would give birth to a son. In which case, 25 December is exactly nine months later. And just as Easter is preceded by a period of preparation – Lent – so Christmas also has a period of four weeks, called 'Advent' (meaning 'the coming') – leading up to the day itself.

The Epiphany ('showing') on 6 January celebrates the coming of the magi to visit Jesus shortly after his birth. In some countries this is a more significant feast than Christmas itself, and Christmas, in any case, has only fairly recently come to such prominence. In the Church's calendar Pentecost was the most important feast of the year, because it marked the foundation of the Church. Easter came second, and Christmas only third in rank. In the past there was a complex system of ranking, but this has been done away with. Now the more important feast are marked by having attached to them 'vigils' or 'octaves'. 'Vigil' means 'watching', and it refers to the practice of beginning important feasts the night before (a 'day', in the early centuries of the Christian era, lasted from sunset to sunset, not from midnight to midnight) with a service of prayers. An 'octave' (meaning 'eighth') is a continuation of the celebration for a feast over the seven days following, ending with the octave eight days later. Only Christmas and Easter now have octaves, though the term is used in various other contexts, especially that of an 'octave' of prayers for some special purpose.

But, of course, the purpose of the calendar is simply to organise the round of celebrations. The central point of any Catholic's religious life is his or her attendance at mass, and this will be described in the next section.

THE MASS

Two separate aspects of the mass will be discussed in this book. The first is what happens during the service, and why. The second aspect is theological – what Catholics believe is going on. This will be presented in a separate section in this chapter (see pp. 110ff.) The mass being described is what is called the 'missa normativa', or the basic service – one without, as you might say, any frills. 'Frills' might include the use of incense, for instance, or more than one priest celebrating at the same time, or the mass might be said either by a bishop, or with a bishop present but not celebrating, and so on. There are a large number of possible variations even to the 'missa normativa', quite apart from the possibility that the mass is cele-brated according to different 'rites', even within the Western Church – though these are uncommon and many Catholics will not have seen a celebration is anything but the standard Roman rite.

The priest comes to the altar dressed in 'vestments'. Nowadays they are more straightforward than they used to be. They are intended to emphasise that what is about to take place is a formal public ritual, not an informal gathering (and so usually, when mass is said in informal surroundings, which it sometimes is, priests dispense with the vestments except for the stole, which is the symbol of office). The colour of the top vestment, the chasuble, varies according to the nature of the feast being celebrated – it is, for example, red on the feast of martyrs. The priest is usually accompanied by altar-servers, traditionally boys, but increasingly now girls as well. They are sometimes called 'acolytes'.

At the beginning of the service there is a form of preparation: the priest and his congregation repent of their shortcomings, or sins, and ask forgiveness. The early Roman liturgy was performed in Greek, and one bit of Greek survived even into the Latin liturgy at this point: the priest or people said, or sang, 'Kyrie eleison, Christe eleison', Greek for 'Lord have mercy/Christ have mercy'. A hymn is then very often sung or said, the 'Gloria in excelsis' or 'Glory to God in the highest', and the hymn is followed by a prayer, called a 'collect'. The collect will vary with the day of the year and, on the feast day of a saint, will invoke the saint's intercession with God. This prayer ends the preparatory phase of the rite.

Next there follows a series of readings. On Sundays and feast days there are usually three: one from the Old Testament, one from New Testament other than the Gospels, and finally one from the Gospels. The first and second readings are separated by a psalm. The readings are taken from the 'Lectionary', which simply means 'book of readings'. They have been selected so that, over the course of three years of Sunday readings, the whole of the New Testament is read, more or less in sequence: the Old Testament reading is chosen to illustrate one of the other readings, normally that from the Gospel. The sequence of readings is broken for major feasts, when readings particularly appropriate to the occasion are chosen. The priest then delivers a sermon or homily – reflections on what has just been read out.

In the early Church those who were preparing to become Christians, the catechumens as they were called, were allowed to be present up to this point, so this part of the service is called 'the mass of the catechumens'. The end of this part, and the beginning of the next, which is called 'the mass of the faithful', is marked by the saying of the creed (see pp. 1ff.)

After the creed has been recited by all, there come the 'Bidding Prayers' – a series of petitionary prayers (i.e. prayers asking God for something) which are concerned with the immediate needs of people in the congregation, or for the Church at large ('bidding', in this context, comes from the Middle English 'bede', the word for prayer).

Next comes the 'offertory', which marks the entry into the solemn part of the mass. The offertory is exactly what it says: the people in the congregation bring up (offer) the bread and wine which will be used during the service. This ushers in the central part of the service, the 'Eucharistic prayer' (for the meaning of the word 'Eucharist', see p. 110). The Eucharistic prayer has a fairly standard form: it is commonly called 'the canon' of the mass, in the sense of the word canon that we have seen before: unchanging. It is not quite unchanging nowadays. There are several different Eucharistic prayers which may be used. In the very early Church it probably was not at all unchanging, being improvised by whoever was presiding at the service. But certain formulas survived, and became fixed. There will be a 'Sanctus' (a short hymn praising God), a recounting of the events of the Last Supper, with Christ's command, 'Do this in memory of me', and what is technically called an 'epiclesis', calling upon God to send the Holy Spirit to bless the gifts on the altar. This section of the mass ends with a 'doxology' – an expression of praise of God, and an 'Amen'.

Following the canon comes the Communion service. This begins with the Lord's Prayer. It contains prayers for peace and 'a sign of peace' – an act of reconciliation with one's neighbour which usually takes the form of shaking hands with those around one. There is another hymn, the '*Agnus Dei*' ('Lamb of God, who takes away the sin of the world, have mercy on us, bring us peace'), and reception of communion (again, see pp. 110ff.) Mass then ends with another prayer said by the celebrant, and a blessing.

GOING TO MASS

Catholics are required to attend mass each Sunday, and also on certain important feast days. These feast days are known as 'holy days of obligation', i.e. days on which one is obliged to go to church. There used to be a great many of these days, but they have gradually been reduced. Some of the most significant feast days such as Christmas Day or Good Friday were (and even in secular Britain still are) public holidays. The important feast days can vary from country to country: the Feast of the Assumption of Mary into heaven (see p. 134) is still a national holiday in some countries on the continent of Europe, as any one who has tried to buy petrol in France or Spain on 15 August will know!

The obligation to attend mass on Sundays was imposed on Catholics 'under pain of mortal sin', i.e. one would commit a mortal sin if one culpably failed to attend. (A mortal sin is defined as one which will condemn a person to hell if he or she commits it, unless it is repented of in the sacrament of confession.)

THE SACRAMENTS

The traditional definition of a sacrament, in essence going right back to the fourth-century Christian bishop St Augustine of Hippo, is that a sacrament is 'an outward sign of inward grace'. This needs some unpacking. First of all, it is 'an outward sign', it is a visible symbol, something one can see or experience. But the reality which it symbolises is 'inward', that is to say it transforms the person from within. But the real problem is with 'grace'. A great deal has been written about grace. It has been divided up into different types, and theologians have debated at length how it affects a person's free will, and other similar topics. But at its most basic, grace simply means God's presence.

There is a very important sense in which God is present in everything – as the English priest-poet Gerard Manley Hopkins famously put it, 'The world is charged with the grandeur of God'. And God is especially present in Christ, so Jesus himself is the sacrament of God's presence to the world, i.e. he makes God present to the world in a visible form. But in Catholic thought there are some particular actions which, when performed within the context of the Church, convey grace, make God's presence a deeper reality for the individual. These are the sacraments. Through them God enters and transforms the individual who receives the sacrament. The significant feature of sacraments is that the rite itself, the actual performance of the ritual, the power of the action which is performed, confers grace. The technical expression for this in Roman Catholic theology is *ex opere operato*, 'from the action itself performed'.

BOX 6.1   EX OPERE OPERATO

The idea that the ritual itself can confer grace (provided that the recipient is worthy of it and not in a state of total separation from God) seems almost as if the ritual were magic. However, it is an important theological point.

The issue arose in the early fourth century when a group called the Donatists said that ordinations carried out by a particular bishop were not valid because, during a persecution, he had betrayed the faith. This argument was rejected by the Church, and especially, though much later on, by St Augustine.

The reason for this rejection was simple: if the conferral of a sacrament depended on the spiritual state of the one conferring it, no one would ever know whether the sacrament had been conferred or not, because the conferror's spiritual state could not be known for certain. One could, on the other hand, know for certain whether the ritual, the act of conferring the sacrament, had been properly performed. The conferring of grace through a sacrament, therefore, must depend not on the person performing the ritual, but the doing of the ritual itself – *ex opere operato*

The Catholic Church has identified seven of these, and they are discussed below. For a long time there was no 'official' list of the sacraments – some writers taught that there were more, some that there were fewer, than seven. But certainly at least for the last 500 years or so the number of seven has been decided upon, and other would-be sacraments have been demoted, as it were, to the category of 'sacramentals': sacramentals will be briefly discussed at the beginning of the next chapter.

The Roman Catholic Church, and the Orthodox Churches, place a great deal of emphasis on the sacraments, the Protestant Churches rather less so. Traditionally the latter recognise only two sacraments (Baptism and the Lord's Supper – the Eucharist), which were clearly instituted by Christ himself. The other sacraments, especially penance, recognised by the Catholic tradition have been making a comeback in all but the most severely Protestant Churches. There has never been, however, any doubt in any Christian Church that baptism was a sacrament.

BAPTISM

There are two very different notions of baptism operating within the Catholic Church which may not be ultimately incompatible but are certainly not easily reconciled. The traditional view has it that every human being is born in a state of 'original sin'. This is the sin committed by Adam and Eve in the Garden of Eden, and the guilt of it, so the theory runs, has been handed down to all the progeny of Adam and Eve – in effect to all humankind. The stain of this sin barred us all from heaven, and it was Christ's life, death and resurrection which 'redeemed' us from this guilt and made us able to enter heaven. The way we participate in this act of redemption is through baptism, when the stain of the sin is washed away.

That, as I say, is the traditional view, and there are all kinds of problems with it, starting with the existence of an historical Adam and Eve, quite apart from the problem of why a sin committed by them, even if they existed, should be communicated to all who came afterwards. There is also the question of what happens to those who are not baptised. They are, on this view, barred from heaven, but it would be an extraordinarily unjust God who sent them to hell for a sin that was no fault of their own. For this reason, the idea of 'Limbo' was invented, a kind of in-between state, neither the happiness of heaven nor the torments of hell, where the unbaptised go if they have lived upright lives. In fact, believing in the existence of Limbo has never been a requirement of the Catholic faith, and it does not appear, for instance, in the official *Catechism* of the Church.

The modern approach is rather different. Baptism is seen, rather than as a washing-away of sin, more as a rite of initiation into the Church. Or, to be more precise, it is part of the rite of initiation, which includes confirmation and reception of the Eucharist. These are still commonly celebrated together in the Orthodox Churches, and also in the Catholic Church when the person entering the Church is not an infant.

The occasion for receiving adults into the Church is usually at the Easter vigil, the long service on the night before Easter Sunday. The ritual may be carried out by full immersion of the person being baptised, but more usually by pouring water on the forehead and saying at the same time 'I baptise you in the name of the Father, and of the Son, and of the Holy Spirit'. This is the basic require- ment, and it can be carried out by anyone, so long as he or she intends to do what the Church intends by the sacrament. Normally, of course, it is carried out by a priest, and is a much more elaborate ceremony, involving a profession of faith, the naming the person, dressing him or her in new clothes (both of these two last symbol- ising the new life into which the person baptised is being born), and also an anointing with oil.

The question of anointing brings us to the sacrament of confir- mation, of which more in a moment. However, there is one more issue about baptism. As was said a moment ago, the full rite of baptism involves a profession of faith, and clearly babies cannot make a profession of faith – in the rite, the godparents do it on the baby's behalf. Some Protestant theologians have argued that baptism should be delayed until the person is old enough to make the profession of faith or, alternatively, should be re-baptised, the so-called 'believer's baptism', when old enough to know what he or she is doing. Though in the early Church the baptism of adults was the norm, the Catholic Church has stood by the practice of infant baptism, partly because of the belief that baptism was necessary to get into heaven, but also partly because of the Catholic sense that people belong to a community – in the case of infants, to the community of their family – and it is the community which supports and protects the faith of the child as he or she is growing up. This is the support that godparents are explicitly called upon to undertake, alongside the parents.

CONFIRMATION

The difficulty of writing about confirmation is that it is next to impossible to distinguish it, both historically and theologically, from baptism. As it is performed, the usual minister of the sacrament is the local bishop, and it incorporates a laying-on (on the candidate's head) of hands. This gesture, the laying-on of hands, is the usual symbol of invoking the Holy Spirit on someone or something – it is done, for example, by the priest at the epiclesis (see pp. 105f.) This sacrament is seen as the 'strengthening' (this is what 'confirming' means) of the newly-baptised person, or, as in current practice, the young adult. It is often presented as the rite of passage into adulthood. In the original order of things, it was followed by the first reception of the Eucharist, though when the sacrament of confirmation became separated from baptism, the order eventually was reversed, so that the Eucharist was received (and for the most part still is) before confirmation.

EUCHARIST

This is the central sacrament of the Church: the Church is sometimes defined as 'a Eucharistic community'. The word comes from the Greek meaning 'thanksgiving', and according to the New Testament, Christ 'gave thanks' at the Last Supper, the final meal he had with his disciples before his crucifixion. He also said 'Do this in memory of me', and that is exactly what the earliest Christian communities did: they shared a meal which recalled the Last Supper, at which a prayer of blessing was spoken over the bread and wine. These were then distributed to those present. In the course of time the meal element disappeared, and only the ritual form of the re-presentation of the Last Supper remained – the story of the Last Supper is recalled in every Eucharistic prayer.

The early Christians believed, and Catholics still believe, that at the Last Supper Christ identified himself with the bread and the wine over which he spoke the blessing. But the Christ who is present in the Eucharist – how he is present we will go on to discuss – is a Christ who has undergone the crucifixion, and has risen from the dead. It is the Christ who has been 'sacrificed' on Calvary. So the mass, which, as has been said, re-presents these events in a ritual form, is itself a sacrifice, a recalling of Christ's sacrifice. It is not *another* sacrifice, it is the same one re-enacted as an act of remembrance. It is precisely because the mass is a sacrifice that the person who presides over it is called a 'priest' (see p. 114) rather than a 'minister', as he or she is in some non-Catholic Churches.

Many, if not most, Christian Churches insist upon what is called 'the Real Presence' of Christ in the bread and the wine. There is, however, considerable disagreement about the manner of that presence. The Catholic position is that, despite appearances, the bread and the wine are wholly changed into the body and blood of Christ – the term most commonly used is 'transubstantiation'. Some Churches say that the bread and wine remain alongside the body and blood of Christ ('Consubstantiation'). Others prefer to say that Christ's presence is symbolic, or is a presence *for* the individual receiving the sacrament.

One quite practical difference about the different interpretations is what the Churches do with the blessed ('consecrated') elements of bread and wine. The Catholic Church, and some others, will preserve them (or at least, the bread) in a special locked receptacle known as a tabernacle, which often used to be on a church's main altar but is now generally located to one side. Because the Catholic Church believes that the bread in the tabernacle is the body and blood of Christ, it is treated with great reverence. It is also removed on occasions for purposes of worship or blessing, and it is also used to give communion, as it is called, to the sick and the dying. Communion for the sick has a special name – '*viaticum*', or 'food for the journey'. It is being in a position to receive communion that signifies you are part of (literally, in communion with) the Church – which is why the Catholic Church is generally, though not absolutely, unwilling to allow members of other Churches to receive communion at mass.

A final word about the bread and wine, 'the elements' as they are often called: if Christ's Last Supper was a Jewish Passover meal, then he would have used unleavened bread, i.e. bread made without any yeast. The Catholic Church uses unleavened bread for the Eucharist: the bread is usually in the form of round disks called 'hosts', though some Churches prefer to use ordinary bread as being more symbolic of a meal. The wine that is used is ordinary wine. Grape juice is prohibited!

The Eucharistic service with communion, then, is the central and most solemn act of Catholic worship, as it is of other Churches. It has to be approached with reverence, and in good standing with God and the Church; which is where the sacrament of reconciliation or, as it is often called, penance or confession, comes in.

PENANCE

We have seen that grace is God's presence to the individual, or his indwelling. But the Catholic Church, as do most other Christian Churches, teaches that human sinfulness puts the individual at a distance from God or, as in the case of the most serious sins – mortal sins as they used to be called – cuts him or her off from God entirely. But Christians believe that God forgives those who repent. The sacrament of reconciliation is the outward sign of that forgiveness. It is, however, rather more than that. The Church believes (and here it parts company from many Protestant Churches) that, acting in Christ's name, the Church itself can administer God's forgiveness. This conviction is based on various texts from the New Testament, but especially a quotation from the Gospel of John: 'If you forgive the sins of any, they are forgiven' (John 20:23).

The history of the sacrament of penance/reconciliation is complicated, but it is important to understand the broad outline. It seems certain that in the early Church forgiveness of serious sin committed after baptism (baptism forgives all sins) was regarded as a once-in-a-lifetime affair. But this was because baptism was administered late in life, and the sacrament of reconciliation was reserved only for the most serious sins, those which would be publicly known, such as murder, or abandoning the faith (apostasy), or embracing an unorthodox brand of the faith (heresy). Because these sins or crimes were public, so was the act of forgiveness. The sinner seeking pardon had to come before the bishop, and then demonstrate his or her sorrow and repentance by undertaking a long period of probation during which by prayer, fasting or other signs the sinner demonstrated that he or she was truly sorry for what he/she had done. The serious sinner had cut him/herself off from the community through the sin committed. The sacrament of reconciliation, presided over by the bishop as head of the local community, was a means of letting the sinner back into the fold after a public, and appropriately lengthy, period of penitence.

The next stage was much influenced by Irish monks who spread across Europe in the sixth and seventh centuries. On the continent of Europe, and in what was fast becoming England, the Church was an urban affair, dominated by towns with their bishops. In Ireland, however, Church life was based on the monasteries. The monks confessed their sins privately, and a penance was imposed – books have survived laying down a tariff, as it were, of these penances. They could be quite severe, but the sinner was no longer cut off from communion while performing them, as had been the case earlier. These tariffs also indicated a change of attitude on the part of the bishop or, increasingly, a priest who was administering the sacrament. Before, he had been a reconciler of the sinner with the community; now he became a judge, determining the severity of the sin/crime committed, and awarding a penance that was appropriate.

Finally, the priest who was by now seen as a judge came to give 'absolution' to the penitent. That is to say, he declared that the sins had been forgiven. This is something of a development, from reconciling to absolving, but the main features of reconciliation are to be found throughout the history of the sacrament:

1   the admission of sin – confession;
2   a determination not to commit the sin again – 'a firm purpose of amendment' in Church-speak;
3   penance – no longer extended periods of fasting, or pilgrimage, but much more symbolic acts such as saying a number of prayers;
4   declaring the sin forgiven – absolution – and the sinner reconciled both to God and the Church.

So penance is an act of healing. There is a second sacrament which is precisely that, a sacrament of healing, though it used to be called 'Extreme Unction' or the last anointing.

ANOINTING OF THE SICK

We know that there was an act of anointing the sick in New Testament times. It is referred to in the Letter of James (5:15f.). This is not a sacrament of the dying, as it came to be seen. We know that the clergy took oil to the houses of the sick and anointed them with it, and prayed over them. It gradually, however, came to be identified with the 'last rites' performed on someone who was about to die, hence the name by which this sacrament used to be known, 'Extreme – or Final – Unction'. Eventually the Church ruled that the sacrament could be administered only to those who were in danger of death. In the Church of today it has once again been restored to its early meaning, as a sacrament of healing, though the healing is of both body and soul. It remains an appropriate element of the 'last rites', but it cannot be identified as such.

The normal minister of all the sacraments so far discussed is a priest. A priest is consecrated, 'ordained' in Church-speak, to this ministry through the sacrament of Holy Orders, and it is to that sacrament which we must now turn.

HOLY ORDERS

There is a major problem about the theology of the priesthood: the Greek word for 'priest' is never used in the New Testament, except of Jewish or pagan priests. It is never used of Church officials. These are 'presbyters' and 'bishops' – 'elders' and 'superintendents' respectively – but not 'priests'. The word 'priest' is applied only to Christ himself in the Letter to the Hebrews. As remarked above (see p. 111), the term 'priest' is used when sacrifice is involved, but in the very early Church it is not at all clear who presided over the Eucharist. From the very beginning of the second century, however, 'bishops' emerge precisely with that responsibility, but at different places at different times: in Rome, for instance, it was quite late on. By the early third century a structure had definitely emerged. A Church was presided over by a bishop, who was marked out for that office by the laying-on of hands by another bishop, thus constituting the 'apostolic succession' which is described elsewhere (see pp. 39f.) Alongside the bishop were the presbyters, who were ordained by the bishop and who could, if instructed to do so by the bishop, preside at the Eucharist in his place.

As time went on and the Church grew larger, the one church in a town was no longer enough. There were several churches in outlying areas, and although these depended upon the cathedral church in the town, they eventually became 'parishes' served by a presbyter, or priest. No one was at first ordained except to serve in a particular place, but eventually priests were ordained without being responsible for a local community. The status of priest – the rank of one who could preside at the Eucharist – thus became divorced from that of minister – someone who served a community. Ultimately the status of priesthood was seen to be so elevated that men sought ordination even though there was no community for them to serve. It became the norm, for example, that all monks were priests, though a monastic community would have need only for a small number of ordained members.

The result was that there were a great many priests who had no pastoral role. Their purpose was, for example, simply to say mass for the souls of people who had died. The sixteenth-century Reformers thought this an abuse. Instead of the status of priest, they stressed that the whole community was a priesthood, and some men were just delegated to perform certain functions within it. At the same time many rejected the Catholic teaching on the sacrificial nature of the Eucharist, which is why Anglican Orders were declared invalid by Pope Leo XIII in a document of 1896 called *Apostolicae Curae* ('Of Apostolic Care'). Part of the argument is that the Church of England bishops ordaining priests did not intend to ordain a 'sacrificing' priesthood.

The basic outline of the ritual of ordination is similar for both priests and bishops. A bishop presides. The candidate is summoned. The litany of the saints is sung (for litanies, see p. 128), there is a laying-on of hands, an anointing and then an investiture in symbols of office: in the case of a bishop he is invested with his ring, the pointed hat called a mitre, and his pastoral staff or crosier, and in the case of a priest in the clothes he wears for the Eucharist, the stole and chasuble (see p. 104). Once a priest or a bishop is ordained he remains ordained for life, in the eyes of the Catholic Church.

This is a natural consequence of the distinction between role (which can be removed or voluntarily abandoned), and status – a distinction which, as we have just seen, developed quite late. When a priest gives up his ministry, after receiving the necessary permission from Rome (which is very hard to get), he is said to be 'reduced to the lay state' – a not very complimentary phrase as far as the laity goes, but one which rather reflects the hierarchical thinking that is typical of the Church. Nevertheless, he is officially considered still to be a priest, but with the obligations of priesthood (celibacy and saying the office – for the latter, see pp. 126ff.) removed.

WOMEN PRIESTS

Throughout this section, when talking of priests, it has always been 'he': the Vatican (and the Orthodox Churches likewise) is completely opposed to the ordination of women to the priesthood. Several arguments are advanced: tradition (there have never been women priests), the fact that Jesus only chose men as his apostles, and because Jesus was a man only a man can serve as his representative. Those favouring the ordination of women think these arguments very weak. Tradition, they would say, is a developing thing and in any case some think that women did exercise priestly functions in the very early Church and perhaps, though this is more dubious, in the middle ages; Jesus had many followers who were women, and the fact that they did not emerge into quasi-leadership roles reflects only the social conditions of the age; and why limit the representative (or 'iconic') aspect of the priest to that of gender – why not say that a priest, to mirror Christ, must also be Jewish as Christ was? At least for the time being, however, Pope John Paul II has determined there will be no women clergy in the Catholic Church, declaring they are not able to be ordained – insisting, in other words, that it is a theological decision to forbid them ordination, and not simply a disciplinary one.

Finally, in this discussion of Holy Orders, attention has been focused on ordination to the priesthood and to the episcopate. Deacons (see p. 64) also receive the sacrament at their ordination. There used to be several other orders (see p. 61), but in the Catholic Church these ranks have now been abolished, and they were not in any case generally regarded as part of the sacrament. The sacrament of orders was, and is, restricted to deacons, priests and bishops. It is the duty of priests and bishops, in normal circumstances, to carry out the sacraments. There is, however, one sacrament which is carried out always by lay people: the sacrament of marriage.

MATRIMONY

As the phrase 'reduced to the lay state' indicates, the Catholic Church, whatever it may now want to insist to the contrary, for a long time regarded the (generally celibate) priesthood as a higher calling than that of marriage. This rather reflects the ambiguities of the New Testament, in particular the letters of Paul. There was an expectation that the end of the world was at hand, and, given that conviction, Christians believed it was better to live in a state of chaste bachelorhood. When the expected end did not happen, the early Christians got on with their normal lives, but some influential figures – St Augustine of Hippo among them – were worried by sexuality. They were convinced it existed solely for the necessary procreation of children, even to the point where any act of inter-course which was not open to the procreation of children was sinful. Sexual intimacy, simply as an expression of love between a husband and wife, was not considered lawful.

Despite this negative view of sexual relations even within marriage, marriage was thought of as a sacrament. But it was not a sacrament administered by a priest: rather it was administered by the partners in a marriage to each other. While this remains the teaching of the Catholic Church, from the end of the sixteenth century it came to be a requirement of a Catholic marriage that it be performed in front of a priest and two witnesses. Notice that this is true of marriages in which one or both partners are Catholics. Marriages where neither partner is a Catholic, and which are not entered into before a priest, are none the less regarded by the Church as being perfectly valid. This is equally true for marriages between non-Christians, or marriages contracted in a registry office. It makes no difference. They are, in Catholic eyes, true marriages – and just as indissoluble as one contracted in front of a priest by two Catholics.

For the Catholic Church regards marriage as a permanent state. It does not approve of divorce and remarriage. To be more precise, it approves of divorce as a necessary civil procedure, but one which does not of itself alter the bond between a man and a women who have been properly married in civil law or in Church law.

ANNULMENT

Nevertheless, marital breakdown is as much a fact of life among Catholics as it is among non-Catholics. For Catholics whose marriage has broken down irrevocably, the only way they can be remarried in a Catholic Church is if they seek an annulment of the first marriage. They have to be able to show to the Church (and each diocese has a tribunal to deal with these problems) that the first marriage was not a marriage in the eyes of the Church. There are a number of reasons why a union may not be a proper marriage. The most obvious is non-consummation: a marriage is not a marriage, the Church says, until the partners have consummated it, i.e., they have had sexual intercourse. Non-consummation may be unusual, but it is certainly a reason for saying there has been no marriage; even the civil courts would agree on that.

More commonly, there is what is called a lack of 'canonical form', that is to say, there was a wedding to which at least one of the partners was Catholic, but it was not performed, as the Church requires, before a Catholic priest (or where there was a dispensation given by the Church to be married in some other way). The Church also requires that a marriage be open to the possibility of having children. If the partners determine beforehand they are not going to have children, this will, as far as the Church is concerned, invalidate the marriage.

The most common reason for declaring a marriage invalid, however, is what is called 'lack of due discretion'. This means that, when the marriage was entered into, one or other, or possibly both, parties were not capable of undertaking the commitment which marriage requires. There are all shades and varieties of this, and the fact that it is allowed at all indicates how seriously the Church regards the obligations entailed when entering the married state, and how important it thinks the commitment of a man and woman to each other to be. It also takes it seriously, and claims authority over marriage, because marriage is a sacrament.

When marriages break down, and one of the partners seeks an annulment, most cases are dealt with by that person's local diocese, though in some rare instances they may be referred to the Vatican. The tribunal in the Vatican is called the Rota.

It is rather depressing to dwell so long on marital breakdown and the Church's method of coping with it, but it is an area of much confusion. To go through all the permutations would take a whole book – and there are indeed several such books. What one should say about the Church's attitude to marriage today is that it is much more positive than it used to be. In the past there was much talk of the 'primary and secondary ends' of marriage, with the begetting of children seen as the primary end, the main purpose of marriage. Now the Church avoids this kind of talk, and although still stressing the importance of children to a marriage, it treats the cultivation and expression of love between the partners as at least equally important.

SUMMARY

1 Catholic worship is centred on the mass, and is organised around an annual cycle, called the calendar.

2 Catholics are expected to attend mass at least once a week.

3 The mass consists of hymns, readings and prayers.

4 The central act of the mass is the 'Eucharistic prayer' (the 'canon'), which recalls the institution of the Eucharist at the Last Supper.

5 The Eucharistic prayer is followed by Communion.

6 There are seven sacraments, traditionally defined as 'outward signs of inward grace'.

7 The sacraments of initiation are:

   a   baptism;

   b   confirmation;

   c   the Eucharist (i.e., in this sense, the reception of Communion)

8 The remaining sacraments are:

   a   penance (or reconciliation);

   b   the anointing of the sick (for healing, but also in preparation for death);

   c   holy orders (for the ordaining of Catholic deacons, priests and bishops);

   d   matrimony (which is regarded as being a life-long commitment).

FURTHER READING

On worship:

The *Catechism*, pp. 247–75.

O'Brien: *Catholicism*, pp. 1063–74.

On the Mass:

The *Catechism*, pp. 453–73.

O'Brien: *Catholicism*, pp. 820–30.

O'Collins, *Catholicism*, pp. 247–69.

On the Sacraments:

The *Catechism*, pp. 255–9.

O'Brien: *Catholicism*, pp. 787–800.

O'Collins, *Catholicism*, pp. 293–6.

On baptism:

The *Catechism*, pp. 276–88.

O'Brien: *Catholicism*, pp. 805–16.

O'Collins, *Catholicism*, pp. 236–45.

On confirmation:

The *Catechism*, pp. 289–96.

O'Brien: *Catholicism*, pp. 816–20.

O'Collins, *Catholicism*, pp. 245–7.

On the Eucharist:

The *Catechism*, pp. 297–317.

O'Brien: *Catholicism*, pp. 820–30.

O'Collins, *Catholicism*, pp. 247–69.

On penance:

The *Catechism*, pp. 319–34.

O'Brien: *Catholicism*, pp.835–43.

O'Collins, *Catholicism*, pp. 270–80.

On the anointing of the sick:

The *Catechism*, pp. 335–42.

O'Brien: *Catholicism*, pp. 843–8.

O'Collins, *Catholicism*, pp. 280–3.

On Holy Orders:

The *Catechism*, pp. 343–57.

O'Brien: *Catholicism*, pp. 863–77.

O'Collins, *Catholicism*, pp. 283–8.

On matrimony:

The *Catechism*, pp. 358–71.

O'Brien: *Catholicism*, pp. 852–63.

O'Collins, *Catholicism*, pp.288–93.

7

DEVOTIONAL LIFE

Ask ordinary Catholics what they believe, and they may be hesitant to answer. Ask them what they *do* as Catholics and you are much more likely to get a clear-cut response. We have seen some of the things which Catholics *do*, such as going to mass on Sundays, receiving the sacraments and the like. Of course, all these things imply much about *belief* as well as about practice, but it is quite likely that many, if not most, Catholics would not be able to give a very coherent theological explanation for what they do. Catholicism is very much a *lived* religion.

It is in that context that we come now to look at the devotional life of Catholics, the kind of religious practices in which Catholics engage outside the formal structures of the liturgy. They add variety to the life of Catholics. And they also add colour. This chapter, for instance, will mention images, pictures or statues, which commonly decorate Catholic churches, Catholic schools and other institutions, and, sometimes, even private houses. It is typical of Catholicism to engage all the senses in the Church's devotional life. Inside a church, for example, there will normally be statues and pictures, and the priest will wear coloured vestments which vary according to the season or feast. There will certainly be music in major ceremonies –

perhaps the medieval 'Gregorian chant', or music written expressly for the celebration of mass by many famous composers right down to the present day. Even the sense of smell may be involved through the burning of incense, an aromatic resin, the smoke of which is said to represent the prayers of the faithful rising to God.

These 'incidentals', as one might call them, to Catholic life are many. They also vary from place to place. In Spain and Latin America, for example, there are often great statue-bearing processions with bands and fireworks on major local feast days. In Britain, on the other hand, processions have almost wholly died out, and even when they occurred in the past they were rather self-conscious affairs. When we come to look at patron saints, to take another example (see pp. 132f.), the saint who is invoked in Italy for help in really difficult situations is St Rita of Cascia, whereas in the English-speaking world the patron saint of 'hopeless cases' is St Jude.

DEVOTIONS

'Devotions', then, are the private religious practices of individual Catholics. They are usually sanctioned by the Church authorities – either by the Vatican or by the local bishop – but they do not necessarily require the presence of a clergyman. Nowadays the liturgy is in the vernacular, but half a century ago in the West it was in Latin: devotional practices for the ordinary Catholic, on the other hand, would for the most part always have been in the vernacular. They are, in a very general sense 'sacramentals'.

SACRAMENTALS

We have seen in the previous chapter that the seven sacraments brought those who received them into the presence of God, the form of presence which in the formal language of theology is called 'grace'. As was then remarked, the significant feature of sacraments is that the rite itself, the actual reception of the sacrament, confers grace. The technical expression for this in Catholic theology is *ex opere operato*. But there are many other means of accessing grace, some of which will be described in this chapter. They, however, are not thought of as conferring grace by the action itself, but because of the disposition of the person performing the action (*ex opere operantis*, i.e. 'from the work of the performer of the action'). It is these actions or rituals which are called sacramentals.

HOLY WATER

The most common example of a sacramental is holy water, which is almost always to be found in little basins ('stoups') at the entrance of churches, and sometimes even in private houses. The stoups contain water which has been blessed by a priest with the sign of the cross. In some pagan Roman, as well as Jewish, rituals water was mingled with a little salt, and this is still the case in the Catholic Church for the formal blessing of Holy Water. It use goes back almost two millennia, though the use of stoups at the entrance to churches has been common for only about half that time: it may originally have had something to do with ritual cleansing before worship. Nowadays Catholics, on entering churches, dip the fingers of their right hand into the water and make the sign of the cross on themselves with their right hand, touching first their forehead, then chest, then left and right shoulders, meanwhile saying 'In the name of the Father, and of the Son, and of the Holy Spirit'.

Holy water is also used in a great many ceremonies which could themselves be called sacramentals, from the blessing of houses to the blessing of a coffin before burial. The use of holy water, it should be said, is not restricted to Roman Catholicism. The Eastern Churches have a similar practice.

PRAYER AND MEDITATION

As the 'sign of the cross' indicates, a worshipper commonly makes a sacramental his or her own by saying a prayer at the same time. Prayer has not been so far discussed, although it is central to Christian life. All liturgical worship consists basically of acts of prayer, the raising of the heart and mind to God in an act of petition. The petition may, and obviously does, vary considerably. In the Eucharist (see p. 106) the celebrant asks God to bless the offerings. In an ordination the prayer petitions God to send the Holy Spirit on to the candidate. In the sacrament of reconciliation the prayer is for forgiveness. But of course prayer extends outside the liturgy into personal appeals to God for health, or for safety, or for passing examinations or, for that matter, anything else that might be deemed appropriate. Catholics are given to praying not only to God, but to the saints. St Anthony of Padua is the patron saint for lost things: Catholics are likely to offer a quick prayer for his assistance in locating mislaid keys or credit cards and so on.

Although prayer has been defined here as petition, it may also take the form of praise of God (and, when sung, hymns). There is a wide variety of different forms of prayers, some of which will be described in the next couple of sections. The basic prayer for all Christians, however, is 'The Lord's Prayer', so called because according to the Gospel of Matthew, chapter 6, it is the prayer which Jesus taught to his disciples.

BOX 7.1   THE LORD'S PRAYER

Our Father, who art in heaven,
hallowed be thy name,
thy kingdom come,
thy will be done, on earth, as it is in heaven.
Give us this day our daily bread
and forgive us our trespasses
as we forgive those who trespass against us.
And lead us not into temptation,
but deliver us from evil. Amen

Also taken in part from the Gospels is the 'Hail Mary', addressed to Mary, Jesus's mother (for devotion to Mary, see pp. 133f.), though the full form as it is used today comes only from about the fifteenth century.

BOX 7.2   THE HAIL MARY

Hail Mary, full of grace,
the Lord is with thee,
blessed art thou among women,
and blessed is the fruit of thy womb, Jesus.
Holy Mary, Mother of God
pray for us sinners now,
and at the hour of our death. Amen

Obviously, anyone is able to make up his or her own form of prayer, but a large number of prayer formulas have been constructed down the centuries – some of them are indeed very old – and are commonly gathered together in prayerbooks.

These formula prayers are meant for saying in common, or at least aloud, though they could also be recited silently. But there is also silent prayer, properly so called, or 'meditation'. There are many forms of meditation, often associated with a particular tradition of silent prayer belonging to one or other religious order: they are often referred to as 'schools of prayer'. In a meditation an individual reflects upon the words of scripture, the life of Christ, the teachings of Christ or of the Church, and by thinking about these things, the meditator hopes to move his or her mind and heart to a love for, and praise of, God. Someone deeply steeped in meditative prayer may find him or herself emptying the mind of all speculative thought and arriving at a state of union with the God to whom they are praying. This higher form of prayer is called contemplation, or sometimes mystical prayer. Prayer at this level, however, is uncommon.

Prayer is, of course, not a specifically Catholic, or even a Christian, activity. It is to be found in most if not all religions of the world. And the techniques of prayer, the means of keeping one's mind turned to God, the positions to adopt, even the style of praying such as the constant repetition of certain words or phrases, all these are to be found in the main religious traditions. Eastern religious techniques, especially those drawn from certain forms of Buddhism, have recently been adopted by many Catholics to help them to pray.

DIVINE OFFICE

Prayer, then, can be said at any time, and in any posture which the one praying finds comfortable. There is, however, a special form of prayer which is meant to be said (or sung) in common, and at particular hours of the day. This is called the 'divine office', and is an obligation on all priests and on communities of monks and nuns, though the manner in which the obligation is fulfilled may vary from community to community. It is part of the formal liturgy of the Catholic Church and is, or should be, performed in public in cathedrals as well as in monastic communities.

The idea of saying prayers at fixed times of the day is something Christianity took over from Judaism. The Office was divided into eight 'hours' of prayer – they are outlined in the accompanying box.

BOX 7.3   TRADITIONAL DIVISION OF THE DIVINE OFFICE

Mattins:	early morning prayer
Lauds:	morning prayer – originally attached to Mattins
Prime:	at the 'first hour', i.e. c. 6.00 a.m.
Terce:	at the 'third hour'
Sext:	at the 'sixth hour'
Nonce:	at the 'ninth hour'
Vespers:	the evening service ('evensong')
Compline:	at bedtime;
Prime, Terce, Sext and Nonce were known as the 'Little Hours'.	

All this was much simplified in 1971. Mattins was replaced by an 'Office of Readings' which could be said at any time during the day; the 'Little Hours' were replaced by mid-day prayer, while vespers and compline were retained.

The basic form of the office is the recitation of the 'psalter', the Book of Psalms. In the traditional form of the office, the whole of the psalter – 150 psalms – was read or sung in the course of one week. Now it is spread over a whole month, thus considerably shortening the amount of time needed. In addition to the psalms, there are prayers, hymns and readings from the Scriptures.

The Office, then, is a very ancient form of prayer within the Catholic Church. Clearly the form which it took, as outlined in the box, reflects its development as a particularly monastic style of worship. The monastic, and the cathedral, form of the office could of course be followed also by lay people, should they so wish, and in time an office was developed for them. It became customary for the more devout (and literate) to say the 'Little Hours', which were little because they were very much shorter. There also evolved the 'Little Office of Our Lady', in which the hymns and prayers were addressed to Mary. This also is quite ancient: its existence is known from the tenth century at least. It did not vary with the seasons and feast days as much as did the full form, and was therefore easier to follow, even to remember by heart – an important factor when many people could not read.

LITANIES

As we have seen, the Divine Office is part of the Catholic Church's official worship. So, once, was the form of prayer called 'Litanies', which go back at least to the fourth century, in the Eastern Church. There they were part of the mass, said after the Gospel where the 'bidding prayers' now occur (see p. 105). Indeed, the litanies fulfilled the same sort of function as the bidding prayers. The deacon would ask the congregation's prayers for various classes of people, and after each petition (the word 'litany' comes from the Greek meaning 'petition') the congregation would call out 'Lord have mercy'.

This was a very simple and straightforward form of prayer, and it was readily adapted in particular to processions, especially to processions which were penitential in nature, when people were expressing sorrow for their sinfulness and asking God's forgiveness and protection. They evolved from a few invocations to a great many, calling upon God, Christ, the Virgin Mary and, eventually, many of the saints of the Church, including holy men and prophets from the Old Testament. In fact the litany is now generally referred to as the Litany of the Saints. It is said, for example, during the ordination of priests.

The form of the litany is, as has been indicated, very simple, and lends itself to numerous variations. A number of different litanies can be found among collections of prayers. The best-known of these is in honour of Mary, and is known as the Litany of Loreto, after a shrine in Italy.

THE ROSARY

The attraction of the litany of the saints is its simplicity. It is easy to remember, or, at least, it is easy to respond to it when someone reads out the invocation. It is also simplicity which accounts for the popularity of the rosary, the most widespread Catholic devotion. To pray the rosary, a Catholic repeats ten 'Hail Marys', which are preceded by an 'Our Father' and followed by the doxology, a prayer of praise to God. (This is strictly speaking the 'Lesser Doxology'.

The 'Greater Doxology' is the *Gloria in excelsis* which is said, or more properly sung, at mass.)

BOX 7.4   THE DOXOLOGY

Glory be to the Father
And to the Son
And to the Holy Spirit
As it was in the beginning
Is now
And for ever shall be, world without end. Amen

The ten 'Hail Marys' are called decades, and there are five decades to a set of rosary beads, on which the person praying counts the number said. It is not simply a matter of repetition, however. While praying the rosary a Catholic is expected to reflect upon, or meditate upon, events of Christ's life. In this context the events are rather oddly called 'mysteries', though there is nothing mysterious about them. The 'mysteries' are divided up into four sets: five Joyful mysteries, recalling Christ's birth and early life, five mysteries of Light, on Christ's public life (these were added by Pope John Paul II in 2002), five Sorrowful mysteries, recalling his passion and death, and five Glorious mysteries, remembering the events of Christ's resurrection. The final 'glorious mystery' is the Coronation of Mary in heaven, which is certainly not something to be found in the New Testament but is a pious belief.

In total, therefore, someone saying a complete rosary will repeat the Hail Mary 200 times (four sets of mysteries times five decades times ten Hail Marys). Until the change in 2002 there were 150 Hail Marys and, as has been remarked above when talking of the Divine Office, there are 150 psalms. It is quite likely that the rosary was modelled on that: it is sometimes called the psalter of the Blessed Virgin. Priests who, for one reason or another, were not able to pray the office, were expected instead to say the full rosary. Incidentally, it is also likely that the idea of the beads as a means of keeping count was taken over from Islam.

Although the rosary is designed as a private devotion, it is often combined with the act of worship known as 'Benediction', or

'Benediction of the Blessed Sacrament'. In this service a host which has been consecrated during mass is put into a display case, called a 'monstrance', then hymns are sung and prayers are said. The service is an act of worship of the person of Christ in the Sacrament, and ends with a blessing (hence 'Benediction') by the priest with the monstrance. As it is a service in praise of Christ, it is a little incongruous that the rosary is commonly said during Benediction, but it is none the less the case.

STATIONS OF THE CROSS

One other devotion which it is important to mention, because any visitor to a Catholic church will see evidence of it, is the stations of the cross. Within a church the 'stations' are usually constituted by a series of fourteen pictures, showing the final stages of Christ's life leading up to the crucifixion. In the past the sequence of scenes has varied, but now it commonly starts with the trial of Jesus before the Roman governor of Palestine, Pontius Pilate, and ends with the laying of Christ's body in the tomb. People who pray the stations will usually move between each of the pictures, say a prayer and reflect or meditate for a while on the part of the story of Christ's passion which is depicted.

Though the origin of this devotion is not entirely clear, it seems to have arisen from the practice in some places of building a representation of Christ's last journey, so that people who could not go on pilgrimage (for pilgrimage, see p. 135) could to some extent follow the experiences of those who had journeyed to Jerusalem. A good number of these 'calvaries', as they were called, still survive, but obviously they were fairly considerable structures. By the end of the sixteenth century representations of the events, or 'stations' of Christ's road to Calvary, were to be found in the rather simpler form of pictures inside churches.

STATUES

In addition to the pictures depicting the stations of the cross, a visitor to a Catholic church is likely to notice the statues, often with a bank of candles burning in front of them. Candles – and statues themselves – are something which tends to mark off Catholic churches from

Protestant ones. The sixteenth-century reformers did not approve of statues in churches – as any visitor to an English cathedral where the heads have been knocked off statues will be aware. The veneration shown to statues seemed to them too much like the worship of idols.

Catholics say that statues are not themselves venerated, but rather are reminders of people who deserve our veneration. These are usually the saints, and especially Mary the mother of Jesus. Sometimes the statues are of Christ. There is always, of course, a crucifix – the depiction of Christ on the cross – on the altar, but there are sometimes statues of Christ the Good Shepherd, an image drawn from the Gospels, and very frequently a statue of the 'Sacred Heart'. This will be instantly recognisable: a figure of Christ, usually with arms outstretched, with a red heart rather garishly emblazoned on the statue's chest. Devotion to the Sacred Heart, though it goes back to the middle ages, became more prominent in the life of Catholics from the mid-seventeenth century. It is a symbol of Christ's love.

The saints depicted in statues vary from place to place. There is commonly an image of the saint after whom the church is named, perhaps a saint who is local to the area, and, where there is a large community from a particular place, a statue of a saint who somehow represents that community. Thus it is common to find, in areas where there is a large Irish community, a statue of St Patrick who converted the Irish to Christianity.

SAINTS

This leads on to the veneration of saints, which is a marked feature of Catholicism. The cult of saints is a vast subject: here there is space only for a brief description. Saints are men and women whose fame as Christians has made them objects of public veneration. 'Public' is important: one often hears said that somebody or other 'is a saint', but no one means that there ought to be public celebration of the fact. The Catholic Church (and some other Orthodox Churches) recognise formally that someone has lived an heroically Christian life, and deserves recognition on that account. This process of recognition is called 'canonisation', a procedure now controlled by the Vatican's Congregation for the Causes of Saints.

The process of canonisation is usually long-drawn-out, and consists of a number of stages. The Congregation first accepts that a person is worth considering for canonisation: at this stage the individual is given the title 'Venerable'. Then there is an investigation into the person's life and writings (if any), to ensure that he or she did indeed exhibit signs of holiness beyond the ordinary, and was not guilty of any deviation from the faith. Unless the person is a martyr, the Congregation requires that a miracle be performed through the intercession of the candidate for canonisation. If all is in order, the person is declared a 'Blessed', which allows him or her to be given public veneration in the Church. Originally the title of 'Blessed', which was only introduced in the seventeenth century, was intended for those to whom there was meant to be only a local cult, but in practice it has become a stage on the way to full canonisation, for which another miracle is required. Miracles are a highly controversial topic, and will be discussed below.

It is important to remember that the process of canonisation as it now exists is a late development. The vast majority of people who are called saints became saints in the first millennium of Christianity, and did not go through this procedure. Their contemporaries thought them holy, and therefore powerful with God, and as a consequence sought their protection. Those who were judged powerful in this way were, first of all, the martyrs, those who in the centuries of persecution died as witness to the faith – 'martyr' comes from the Greek and means 'witness'. Some people were imprisoned for their faith but, despite their sufferings, did not die: they were called 'confessors', again a word, in Latin this time, meaning 'witness'. The terms 'confessor' and 'martyr' are still used to distinguish the categories of saints. Gradually the concept of confessor was extended to include those whose extraordinary lives seemed to demonstrate the power of God in their lives, and therefore their power with God. This notion of 'power' with God is demonstrated, in the eyes of Catholics, by their ability to work miracles (a power more obvious in the past, it has to be said, than in modern times), and therefore their appropriateness as intercessors before God.

Though perhaps rather less thought is given nowadays to the miracle-working power of saints, the notion of saints as protectors has remained. Some saints are regularly invoked by certain Catholics for protection in particular situations – from thunderstorms, for example, or from fire. These are known as 'patron' saints. Most professions have their patron (that of writers, for instance, is St

Francis de Sales); so do countries. St Rose of Lima, for example, is perhaps not surprisingly the patron saint of Peru, while St Anthony of Padua who, despite his name, was born in Portugal, is the patron saint of that country.

Some people are much devoted to saints, others not so, but their function within the Church is an indication of one of the important beliefs of Catholicism. For Catholics there is no final boundary between death and life. Catholics, like all Christians, believe in life after death. Christians commit themselves to a belief that there is a 'bodily' resurrection for all, just as Christ himself rose from the dead, though just what that means is a matter for much discussion. It does however imply that people survive as individuals and are not just absorbed into some greater totality of being.

There is, then, for Christians a continuity between this life and the next. Catholics talk about 'the communion of saints', meaning a community of the Church in which some are in heaven ('the Church triumphant'), some are still working out their salvation on earth ('the Church militant'), and some are ridding themselves in Purgatory of the guilt for the sins which they have committed during life ('the Church suffering; about the idea of Purgatory, see pp. 136ff.) One sign of this continuity is that the 'feast day' of a saint, the day on which his or her life is commemorated, is usually the day of the saint's death – because this is his or her 'birthday' into heaven.

MARY, MOTHER OF JESUS

Among the saints, Mary the mother of Jesus has a special place in Catholic, and in Orthodox, devotion, and though veneration of her was played down by the first generation of Protestant reformers it did not entirely disappear in the mainstream Churches of the Reformation. The long and complicated story of the development of the devotion need not be gone into here, but it is important to remember that, although the place Mary has been given has its origins very early on in Christian history, it has a great deal to do with defending Christian teaching on the nature of Christ himself.

For instance, it has been the constant teaching of the Church that Mary was a virgin before giving birth to Jesus, and it is Catholic tradition that she remained a virgin for the remainder of her life.

However, the Gospels, though they *may* indicate Mary was a virgin, do not expressly say so: the interpretation put on the text was to defend Christ's divinity. It is central to the Christian faith that Jesus is God: if Joseph, Mary's husband, had been his father then Christ's divinity might not have been so evident. Hence Mary is almost always referred to in Catholic circles as 'the virgin Mary' or, more commonly, 'the blessed virgin Mary' which is often abbreviated to BVM. But in order to defend Jesus's godhead, one early council of the Church proclaimed that, because Mary was Jesus's mother, she was Mother of God (or *'theotokos'* in Greek, meaning 'God-bearer').

Mary's virginity is frequently confused with the belief in her 'immaculate conception'. This latter refers to Mary's own birth, not to Jesus's birth, and implies that Mary was herself kept free from original sin. This was a controversial doctrine in the middle ages, but by the mid-fifteenth century it had become widely accepted. In 1854 it was declared a dogma. The only other officially declared dogma, pronounced in 1950, is that of Mary's assumption into heaven. That Mary was taken body (again, whatever exactly that might mean) and soul into heaven has a longer history than that of the immaculate conception. As with the virginity of Mary, there is no scriptural proof of it, though it has been a longstanding tradition. When it was declared a dogma, the Pope of the time made no attempt to specify what it might mean in detail.

The immaculate conception, the assumption and several other events such as the nativity of Mary, are celebrated as feasts of the Church. But Mary is also known under a variety of different titles, such as Our Lady of Lourdes, Our Lady of Guadalupe – a feast much celebrated in Latin America – Our Lady of Loreto and so on. These titles usually derive from shrines of the BVM in different parts of the world, and it is to shrines in general that we now turn.

SHRINES, PILGRIMAGES AND MIRACLES

The word 'shrine' comes from the Latin *scrinium*, meaning a chest or set of drawers in which books and papers were kept. Eventually such chests were used to hold the bones, or other relics, of saints. In the middle ages it was regarded as important if one wanted to solicit the patronage of a saint to be as near as possible to her or him. Ideally this meant being at, or near, the place where the saint was buried – the most obvious example being the basilica of St Peter's in Rome, which was thought to be, and probably was, built by the Emperor Constantine over the grave of the Apostle Peter.

So a shrine is a holy place associated with a saint, either through the presence of relics, or of an image (often supposed to be miraculous), or the site of an 'apparition'. An apparition is the appearance of some holy person, usually the Virgin Mary, to an individual or a group of individuals, usually accompanied by private revelations. Such sites are not uncommon – Fatima in Portugal and Lourdes in France are two of the best-known appearances of Mary. It should be said that, although the Church will approve of feast days (the feasts of Our Lady of Lourdes, or of Our Lady of Fatima for example) and of devotion to Mary under those titles, it has been much more reticent in committing itself to the reality of the appearances themselves.

Shrines do not exist in isolation. They are the focus of religious devotion which may be purely local, or it may be international. People travel to these shrines, sometimes over long distances. The most obvious shrines are those in the Holy Land (Palestine/Israel) associated with the life of Christ. We know that people went to the Holy Land to visit these sites as early as the third century, and in the fourth century the Emperor Constantine's mother, St Helena, went there and had churches built at some of the most significant places. Around AD 380 a Spanish nun, Egeria, visited the Holy Land and left an account of her pilgrimage.

The idea of pilgrimages, of travel to holy places, is not limited to Christianity – there is of course, in Islam, the famous pilgrimage to Mecca which every Muslim is expected to make at least once – but within Christianity, or more specifically within Catholicism, it became a major phenomenon in the middle ages. Pilgrimages were imposed as a form of penance. They could be pilgrimages to the Holy Land, or to Rome, or to the shrine of the Apostle James at Santiago in northwest Spain ('Santiago' is Spanish for St James). But there were many other pilgrimage destinations, including some in England, most famously perhaps that of Canterbury, the site of the martyrdom in 1170 of Thomas Becket immortalised by Chaucer in the *Canterbury Tales*.

Pilgrims did not simply visit shrines as an act of penance, however. They went there as well seeking a saint's miraculous intervention: a saint's power, as has already been remarked, was thought to be greatest where his or her body, or at least its relics, were to be found. Miracles are one of the more controversial aspects of Catholicism. They can be defined as the special intervention of God (when saints 'work' miracles, they do so, Catholics believe, only because of their intercession with God) leading to the suspension of the normal course of nature. Most commonly they take the form of sudden cures when medical remedies had proved unsuccessful, though that need not be the case. For instance, there have been examples of miraculous intervention, so it is claimed, to ensure that the supply of food did not run out. Miraculous cures have often been claimed by visitors to Lourdes, some of which have, after scientific examination, been shown to be inexplicable in the current state of human knowledge.

Though nowadays many people go on pilgrimage (the 'camino' or road to Santiago from Roncesvalles on the Franco–Spanish border is walked by many thousands each year) simply for devotional reasons, in the past they often went seeking miracles. Indeed, some people still visit shrines, especially that of Lourdes, hoping for a miracle cure. But for many the difficult and often dangerous journey was an act of penance for some sin they committed, and this brings us finally to one of the most problematic features of Catholicism, the doctrine of indulgences.

INDULGENCES

If a single cause were to be cited as the origin of the early sixteenth-century disputes within the Church which led to the Reformation, it would be the doctrine of indulgences. It seemed to the reformer Martin Luther that the Church was selling the forgiveness of sin through the sale of indulgences. The notion of an 'indulgence' is a difficult one, and moreover it is associated with the doctrine of purgatory, something which the Reformers also questioned.

In Catholic thought, although a sin may have been forgiven through the sacrament of reconciliation, punishment for that sin remains. This punishment is 'purged' in a state called purgatory, which sinners enter after death in order to be made perfect so that they can enjoy union with God in heaven. People are in purgatory until they have been cleansed of all the guilt of the sins they have committed during their lives. It is a Catholic belief that 'the souls in purgatory', as the expression is, can be speeded on their way to heaven by the prayers of those on earth. It is, therefore, quite proper in Catholicism to pray *for* the dead as well as *to* (the dead) saints. Christians have prayed for the dead from the earliest centuries, something which appears only to make sense when accompanied by some sort of a doctrine of purgatory, but it is difficult if not impossible to deduce the existence of such a state, or place, from the Scriptures. Hence the Reformers' antipathy towards it.

The doctrine on indulgences is closely linked to purgatory because it was – and is – believed that some of the guilt remaining after a sin has been forgiven can be remitted by penitential practices such as a pilgrimage. When 'indulgences' were granted, they were calculated, as it were, in relation to so many days, weeks or even years of a suitable penance. Although Catholics often thought of an indulgence as letting one off so many days or weeks of purgatory, that was not really the theory: one was commuting the punishment by so many days, weeks or years of penance.

However, there came into being, especially in the context of the crusades from the end of the eleventh century, the idea of a 'plenary' indulgence, an indulgence which remitted all the guilt remaining for sins committed, thus seeming to guarantee immediate entrance into heaven at death. The offer of such indulgences has been cited as one of the reasons why noblemen were so ready to go off to the Holy Land to fight Muslims and regain possession from them of the Holy Places.

This book is concerned to describe and explain Catholicism, not to defend it, and certainly not to attempt to summarise the complex theology which lies behind the doctrine of indulgences. As time has gone on, indulgences have become more a means of encouraging devotion, and the practice of counting indulgences in the form of days and weeks has been abandoned. Though the doctrine itself has not been done away with, indulgences play a much smaller part in Catholic life nowadays than they did even half a century ago.

This chapter has been looking at various kinds of devotions. There are very many more of them – those mentioned above are only a small selection. There is, however, one very major act of devotion practised throughout their lives by many thousand Catholic men and women. They take vows.

VOWS

A vow taken in a Catholic context is no different from any other: it is a formal promise to do something – in the middle ages, for example, to go on a crusade, or to make a pilgrimage. Though there can be many kinds of vows, the traditional ones within the Catholic Church are those of poverty, chastity and obedience. They can be taken privately so no-one knows but the person making the vow and perhaps a few others, or taken publicly, or solemnly, in which case everyone knows, or could know. They can be taken as an act of devotion by lay people or by clergy, but most commonly they are taken within the context of religious orders, and before going on to discuss the vows themselves, something has to be said about these.

RELIGIOUS ORDERS

The technical name nowadays for these organisations is 'Institutes of Consecrated Life'. They are groups of men or women (rarely both in the same institute) who live according to a particular rule, or way of life, usually one formulated by the person who founded the order. There is nothing specifically Catholic, or even Christian, about 'monks' as they are commonly, though not always accurately, called. There are monks in Buddhism, for instance, and there is a flourishing tradition of religious life in the Orthodox Churches. Within the last couple of centuries religious life has revived within the Anglican Communion. Monks (and nuns, the female equivalent) are, however, a distinct feature of Catholicism.

The origin of the monastic life, as it is called, is usually attributed to St Anthony (251–356), who went out into the Egyptian desert in order to be alone ('monk' comes from the Greek '*monos*' meaning 'alone'). After a time other people gathered around Anthony, and formed themselves into small communities. These communities are called 'coenobitic', again from the Greek and meaning 'common': their members lived a life in common. Others, however, continued to live alone as hermits – the 'eremitical' life, from the Greek '*eremos*' meaning 'solitary'.

There has been a small, continuing, tradition of people living the life of hermits, and some religious orders have attempted to combine the eremitical with the coenobitic by constructing monasteries in which the monks live in silence, in individual rooms (or 'cells'), or even in small houses with gardens gathered around a common dining room (refectory) and chapel. The Carthusian Order, founded in 1084, is an example of this.

Over time a number of different rules of life were developed. The first person to do so was, it is thought, St Pachomius, who lived in Egypt from the end of the third to midway through the fourth century: he founded his first monastery in about 320. The rule of Pachomius influenced St Basil (330–79), who drew up in the form of questions and answers a kind of catechism about how to live the religious life. It is this which is very largely followed to this day by monks in the Eastern tradition. The best-known rule, however, is that of St Benedict, written in Italy about the year 540. It is the most widely followed, and those monks who do so are known as Benedictines. But it is also used by other orders who have different interpretations of the original rule, or choose to stress different aspect of it. Then there is the rule of St Augustine (356–430). Older than St Benedict's, but not a formal rule, much of Augustine's rule was taken from one of the Saint's letters. This 'rule' was adopted by priests who were influenced by the reform movement of the mid-eleventh century and decided to live their lives in common. They were called 'canons' – 'canon', as we have seen, comes from a Greek word meaning fixed or unchanging. There was an important difference between monks and canons, quite apart from their rule: whereas monks usually lived in the countryside, canons were town dwellers.

In the early thirteenth century another form of religious life emerged: that of the friars. Monks and canons had lived more or less in one place: friars – like canons, largely town-dwellers – moved around and thereby became to some extent better known. (The best-known friar in English mythology, Friar Tuck, one of Robin Hood's 'merry men', could not really have existed: the stories of Robin Hood are set at a time before friars emerged.) Despite moving about, they continued to live in communities and to recite the divine office (see pp. 126ff.) in common.

In the sixteenth century there emerged yet another new concept of the religious life with the founding of the Society of Jesus, or Jesuits. The Jesuits, who received papal approval in 1540, still for the most part lived in communities, but they were geared to leading individual lives with less reliance upon community living and, like priests who belong to dioceses, they said (rather than sang) the office – and did so on their own rather than in common. They certainly moved round a great deal, and were famous for their missionary activity in India, China and, perhaps particularly, in the New World of the Americas. A good many other religious orders were founded with constitutions modelled on that of the Society, a constitution which allowed them to be very active rather than tied down to specific times of prayer. They were (and are) similar to diocesan clergy, but are none the less members of a religious order. They are known as 'clerks regular'.

In 1947 another form of religious, or consecrated (i.e. consecrated or committed to God) life was recognised by the Church, that of secular institutes. These are bodies of people who, as the saying goes, live 'in the world', that is to say, they do ordinary jobs rather than those traditionally associated with nuns or priests, but live a life according to a rule – and often in communities, though not necessarily so.

The above is a summary outline of the development of religious orders in the Catholic Church. There are a great many different orders, and each one has its own structure and way of life. Some institutes which look like religious orders are not orders. There are, for example, a good many associations of priests created to do a particular work whose members do not take the vows – some foreign mission societies, for example, fall into this category.

CHASTITY

What distinguishes institutes of consecrated life, or religious orders, from these associations, therefore, is the existence of vows. Traditionally there are three vows, or formal commitments to God. They are vows of poverty, chastity and obedience. Chastity is the easiest to explain: it is a commitment to abstain from absolutely all sexual activity. This practice is, of course, common in some world religions other than Catholicism, where it is embraced either permanently or for a period of time. In Catholicism (but not necessarily in the Eastern Churches united to Rome) it is also required for all priests, religious or diocesan, though diocesan priests do not take a formal vow of chastity – or celibacy, as it is usually known in this context. However, since

1972 they have been required to make a formal profession of celibacy before their ordination to the deaconate, a preliminary stage on the way to ordination to the priesthood.

The issue of celibacy is a very live one in Catholicism, partly at least because of the decline in the number of clergy, especially in Europe and the Americas. Some people believe that if priests were allowed to marry, then more people (men only, in the present Catholic dispensation) would offer themselves for the priesthood. The obligation of celibacy for the clergy goes back a long way, certainly to the fourth century. Only since the twelfth century have the Church authorities been able to insist on celibacy as necessary for priests in the West, though, as is well known, individual members of the clergy have not always been able to maintain the standards required of them. It is important to remember that celibacy for diocesan clergy is generally held to be a matter of ecclesiastical discipline rather than being of the essence of that particular state of life. It can, therefore, be waived, as it has been, for instance, in the case of some married Anglican clergy who wished to become Catholic priests.

Celibacy is defended on both spiritual and practical grounds – and on a mixture of both (e.g. theoretically at least it enables a priest to devote himself in love to all those whom he is called upon to serve, without having a special relationship with one group, namely his family). It should be remembered, however, that those within the Catholic Church who are critical of the obligation of celibacy are usually critical of it precisely because it is an obligation, and not something freely embraced – as it is within religious orders under the vow of chastity – but imposed on anyone wishing to be a priest. They do not have a problem with the notion of celibacy in itself.

POVERTY

On the face of it, the vow of poverty should also be easy to define. It means having nothing of one's own. However, what this may mean in practice will vary from religious order to religious order. Some embrace a very rigorous interpretation, and depend on gifts for their survival (though this is rare nowadays). In most instances the men and women of the Orders work for a living, one way or another – for instance, teaching in schools, or working in hospitals. Although they earn money, religious may not keep it for themselves: it goes to fund other aspects of an Order's activity which is not self-supporting – working on the missions, for example. Poverty, in almost all cases, does not mean penury: how much money an individual has for his or her own purposes, such as going away on holiday, depends on the specific decision of the governing council of an order, or is laid down in the rule of life.

OBEDIENCE

The same is true for the vow of obedience. This, too, varies according to the interpretation of the rule of life as laid down by the order's founder. What it certainly does not permit is that a superior is able to instruct a member of his or her community to do something which the member believes to be against his or her conscience. Obviously there may be disagreement about some things. There is usually a 'court of appeal', as it were, though instances of this kind of conflict are on the whole rather rare.

RELIGIOUS LIFE

Members of religious orders do not take these vows immediately on entering the order. There is almost always a year, often two years, of preparation, or spiritual formation, at the end of which temporary vows may be taken, which are renewed after a set number of years, though some orders take permanent vows after the two years 'noviceship'. This noviceship, or 'noviciate', is a feature of training which is specific to the orders: those training for the diocesan priesthood do not go through such a stage. After vows, the 'juniors' as they are sometimes called will then put on the 'habit'. The different orders have different styles of dress, though nowadays these have been very largely either simplified, or entirely discarded in favour of the style of the day – though priests often still wear what is called 'the Roman collar', a band of white material around the neck. It used to be the custom for many religious to change their name on taking vows, as a sign of starting a new life. The name chosen was that of a saint, and it could be male or female. Hence the apparent oddity that some nuns had male names – Patrick or Wilfrid, for example.

Subsequent training will depend on what a person is going to do – teach in a school, work in a hospital, go on foreign missions and so on. But some theological education is normally included, and those training for the priesthood will study both philosophy and theology, and very often attend university to get a degree, perhaps in theology but not infrequently in another subject – mathematics or history, for instance. This is true, incidentally, of the diocesan clergy as well as the religious. Of course, not all religious are preparing for the priesthood. Nuns are not, and there are some religious orders of 'brothers' – men who are full religious but do not wish to be ordained. Some orders made up mainly of priests often have brothers among them.

There are a great many orders, some limited to a diocese or group of dioceses, others spread throughout the whole Church. The headquarters, sometimes called 'the mother house', of the major orders are usually in Rome. The orders are very diverse in structure and style of living, and equally diverse in the work which they undertake on behalf of the Church. Some are devoted solely to a life of prayer, and their members rarely if ever leave the houses in which they have taken their vows: they live within the 'enclosure', an area into which no woman (in a male institution) or man (in a female one) may enter. Such orders are called 'contemplative', and are contrasted with the 'active' orders who nurse, teach, research and generally engage with the world about them. The Church's engagement with the world will be the subject of the next chapter.

SUMMARY

1   Sacramentals are distinguished from sacraments because they depend for their efficacy on the disposition of the individual.
    a   Holy (i.e., blessed) water is one of the oldest and most widespread of these
2   The recitation of set, formula-style prayers, or reflection on some religious theme (for example an episode in the life of Christ) in meditation are an essential part of Christian life.
    a   Divine Office is the official prayer of the Catholic Church, obligatory for priests, and – usually – for members of religious orders.
    b   Litanies, calling, for example, upon the saints, or Mary, in a list of petitions, usually followed by the words 'pray for us', occur in some solemn liturgical ceremonies.

    c The rosary, the repetition of simple prayers while meditating upon the life of Christ, is one of the most popular forms of prayer.

3 Aids to prayer are very common, such as statues and other images: the Stations of the Cross is a particular example of this, recalling Christ's passion and death.

4 Saints are also prayed to, some being associated with particular places, things or needs. Patron saints are called upon for protection, or for help in particular cases.

    a Saints were originally created by the devotion to them of the Catholic faithful and their supposed power with God.

    b They are now created through a process called canonisation.

5 Mary, Mother of Jesus, is also a saint, and venerated as such, under a number of different titles such as The Immaculate Conception, or Our Lady of Lourdes or of Fatima.

    a Lourdes and Fatima, and many more, especially the burial places of saints or the places of supposed apparitions, or, particularly, the places associated with the life of Christ, are places of pilgrimage.

    b Traditionally, through pilgrimage, or the saying of certain prayers, Catholics could obtain an 'indulgence', often wrongly interpreted as 'time off' purgatory.

6 Vows, formal commitments to God to live a certain type of life, are another form devotion.

    a Religious orders are organisations within the Catholic Church for men and women leading lives under vows.

    b The traditional vows are:

       poverty: owning nothing of one's own;

       chastity: leading a life without any sexual activity;

       obedience: submission of the will to a religious superior.

    c There are several different types of religious order: monks, friars, clerks regular, each with a different style of life, led under a rule usually, but not always, drawn up by the order's founder.

FURTHER READING

On prayer and devotional life:

The *Catechism*, pp. 372–77, 544–85.

McBrien, *Catholicism*, pp. 1019–57, 1070.

O'Collins, *Catholicism*, pp. 373–6.

Walsh, *A Dictionary of Devotions*, passim (for individual devotions, including pilgrimages).

On saints:

The *Catechism*, pp. 216–22.

Farmer, *Oxford Dictionary of Saints*, pp. vii–xxi.

McBrien, *Catholicism*, pp. 1077–116.

O'Collins, *Catholicism*, pp. 367–73.

Woodward, *Making Saints*, passim (for the process of canonisation).

On purgatory and indulgences:

The *Catechism*, pp. 235, 331–3.

McBrien, *Catholicism*, pp. 1164–70.

O'Collins, *Catholicism*, pp. 221–33.

On the religious life:

The *Catechism*, pp. 211–15.

Day, *Dictionary of Religious Orders*, passim.

O'Collins, *Catholicism*, pp. 49–50, 56–64.

8

THE CHURCH IN SOCIETY

Chapter 6 described the public rituals of Catholic life. The previous chapter to this one has described the more individual, but still for the most part public, activities of Catholic devotion. But Catholics like everyone else have private lives, and these lives are, or ought to be, equally influenced and informed by their faith.

FAMILY LIFE

The family, it is often said, is the first school of the faith, and The *Catechism of the Catholic Church* devotes a good deal of space to the family unit, which, in Catholic thought, is said to be 'the domestic Church'. A family exists for the good of the partners in marriage, but it also exists for the procreation and education of children, and to provide them with a stable environment in which children may grow up. That environment, the Church expects, will include family prayers and certainly family mass-going. For a long time the Church authorities were opposed to 'mixed marriages', i.e. marriages where one partner is a Catholic and the other not. Mixed marriages were discouraged because they appeared to bring division into the heart of the family in the all-important matter of religion. The prohibition was never absolute, but that it existed at all is a witness to the importance which the Church put on family unity. Mixed marriages are no longer regarded as so much of a problem, but the Church makes an effort to ensure that the non-Catholic partner understands the religious attitudes of the Catholic. And both partners undertake so far as possible to bring up the children as Catholics.

It may seem surprising that a Church which, on the face of it, puts so much emphasis on celibacy for its clergy, and in which monks and nuns take the vow of chastity, should also value the family so highly. Of course, there are vastly more married people than there are celibate ones in the Church, but probably the real reason why the family is so highly valued is not so much for religious reasons as for social ones: the family is regarded as the main 'building block' of society. It exists before society, and the Church expects society to foster, rather than to damage, family life. As was explained earlier (see pp. 117ff.), the bond of marriage is thought of by the Church as a natural one, which exists, as an indissoluble union, just as much outside the Church as within it.

Catholicism is strong on communitarian values, and sees the family as the basic community, united in the faith. This is one reason why it promotes the baptism of infants, incorporating them into the Church even though babies are obviously not themselves in a position to make a personal commitment to the faith. But the faith is that of the family as a whole, and then of the community, usually the parish, of which the family is a member. Infant baptism has been the practice from very early times, though some Churches of the Reformation chose to delay the sacrament until the individual was old enough to know what he or she was doing. In the past there was the additional spur to infant baptism in the belief that, because of original sin, anyone who died before baptism could not enter heaven.

CONTRACEPTION

One of the facts about Catholics which is widely known is the Church's opposition to birth control – or, more correctly, opposition to artificial means of birth control. The Church has shown itself well aware of the problem of overpopulation, and is not opposed to the regulation of births, of family planning in other words, in order to mitigate the pressures on natural resources posed by too many people pursuing limited supplies of food and water. But while acknowledging the problem, the papacy in the second half of the twentieth century ruled as immoral the most obvious means of coping with overpopulation through artificial birth control. The opposition was expressed by Pope Paul VI in his 1968 letter to Catholics entitled *Humanae Vitae* ('Of human life'). This letter came as a great surprise. A commission had been established to decide whether modern techniques of contraception could be morally justified. It became widely known that the majority of people on the commission reported in favour of the Church accepting certain forms of birth control ('the pill') as well as so-called 'natural' methods (restricting intercourse to the times of a woman's supposed infertility, something notoriously difficult to judge). When the Pope adopted, instead of the majority report, the conclusions of a small minority of commission members there was an enormous outcry.

The argument against contraception is that it is unnatural, and that it militates against one of the primary ends of marriage, namely the begetting of children. There was also a fear, which was it would seem well-founded, that the prevalence of contraception would foster a climate in which sexual relations outside marriage became a commonplace. The Church's traditional morality, however, regards sexual relations as only permissible within marriage. Whether the Church's teaching will ever change is a matter of debate, but it is clear that the sexual morality of Catholics is little different, as far as the use of contraception is concerned, from that of the population at large. In fact so widely has the prohibition on contraception in *Humanae Vitae* been ignored that it is hard to deny it has undermined papal authority, which is no longer accepted as unquestioningly by Catholics as it was in the first half of the twentieth century.

'PRO-LIFE' ATTITUDES

Unlike contraception, it is generally thought that Catholics remain more opposed to the practice of abortion than do the majority of the population. There is, however, not much evidence that Catholic women have abortions less frequently than do other women. Opposition to abortion stems from the belief that a human life begins at the moment of conception, or at the latest very shortly afterwards, and there is a prohibition on the taking of life. The argument is simple enough, but the situations which arise can be very complicated – for instance, where giving birth might threaten the life of the mother.

These sorts of issue arise in medical ethics in general: euthanasia is a similar case. The Catholic Church is firmly against euthanasia, but the problem is often one of definition. Catholic moral theologians would argue, for instance, that doctors do not have to go to extraordinary lengths to keep someone alive. But where, as it were, is the cut-off point? About that there is much room for disagreement.

BOX 8.1   THE SEAMLESS ROBE

The abortion issue raised emotions high in the United States. Quite often those who were most in favour were also in favour of the death penalty. Cardinal Bernardin of Chicago (d. 1996) argued that life was 'a seamless robe'. If one were against abortion and contraception, he suggested, then one ought logically to be equally against the death penalty and all other forms of violence against life.

Then there is the principle of double effect. While, say the moralists, it is absolutely forbidden to do something which is evil, one may perform an act which has two consequences, one good (which is what is intended) and one bad (which is not intended but is an unfortunate outcome). As far as abortion is concerned, the Church proposes as a general principle that human life begins very early on. But this is not something which is accepted by everyone – not even by all Catholic moralists. It is easy to enunciate general principles in the field of sexual ethics – and indeed in the field of medical ethics in general – but it is less easy to deal with the particular. However, the Catholic Church worldwide has been in the forefront of those who have campaigned against legalising abortion – which brings us neatly to the question of politics.

POLITICS

In a good number of countries of the world the Catholic community constitutes the majority of the population – in many cases the overwhelming majority. In these instances, should the Church attempt to dictate what should, or should not, be the law of the land? In other words, should the moral category of 'sin' become the legal category of 'law'? This is a position called 'integrism', and its protagonists are called by the (French) term *integristes*. To some extent it exists in the USA in the 'Christendom' movement which has set up schools, universities and now even a township where the rules of communal living are, to a great extent, the rules of the Catholic Church. It is also represented in the Tradition, Family and Property movement, which began in Brazil and is widespread in Latin America, though it also exists elsewhere. Significantly, members wear a cloak, reminiscent of medieval dress – the middle ages being the high point of 'Christendom', a world in which the Church exerted enormous influence over people's daily lives.

'Integrism' has two meanings. The first is that which has just been described, where the Catholic Church becomes, as it were, the 'soul' of the civic community. The second meaning is related to the first: it is applied to the cast of mind which makes every aspect of the faith equally significant. So, for instance, there are people who believe that every article of clothing a priest wears to celebrate the Eucharist is just as important a part of the Catholic faith as belief in the presence of Christ in the Eucharist. In other words they attach as much importance to the incidental trappings of Catholicism as they do to the substance of its creed. They are, in other words, in Catholicism what 'fundamentalists' are in Protestantism.

The *integristes* are on the far-right wing of Catholicism, and there are relatively few of them. They are, or were, of political importance because their brand of Catholicism was until the middle of the twentieth century to some extent the official version. Under the slogan 'error has no rights', the Church demanded of governments in countries where there was a dominant Catholic majority that non-Catholic religions should not be allowed to practise their faith publicly. The Church had a say in a whole range of state undertakings, such as marriage laws (the Republic of Ireland, for instance, for a long time had no provision for divorce), education, health-care and so on. In such countries it was often the case that the clergy, especially bishops, sat in the legislature, and clerical salaries were to some extent provided by the state. (In countries where Catholics were in a minority, the Church, of course, demanded toleration, a rather hypocritical stance – as many, even some within the Church, were quick to point out.)

This attitude was formally abandoned at the Second Vatican Council, when the bishops of the Church approved the document called *Dignitatis humanae* ('Of human dignity') which argued for religious freedom for all, rather than just toleration. Although there is mention in this document of the 'confessional' state, the main thrust of its argument is that the state has no jurisdiction in spiritual matters. All it can do, and what indeed it must do, is to guarantee the free exercise of religion, so long as to do so does not infringe anyone's human rights.

Of course, Catholics are expected, and encouraged, to engage in politics as individuals, and to bring their convictions as individuals to bear upon legislation. This does not entirely solve the problem, because what happens when a Catholic is faced by a vote on something, say abortion, where the Church has a clear line? A democratically-chosen representative must in conscience do what he or she thinks appropriate for the good of those he or she represents. After all, most laws are permissive: because it is possible to have an abortion it does not mean that women are *obliged* to have them. These may seem fairly remote matters, certainly from British politics, but they are issues which have surfaced in the United States especially when there have been presidential candidates who are practising Catholics.

There have of course been specifically Catholic parties, even in Western democracies: the Centre Party in Germany and the Popular Party in Italy, for example. The Christian Democrat Parties, which held power in Italy, Germany and in some countries of Latin America, for example, were in origin Catholic parties.

CATHOLIC SOCIAL TEACHING

To say that there have been Roman Catholic political parties suggests that there is a specifically Catholic political agenda. This is not the case, and for two main reasons. First of all, though Catholics may possibly agree about *ends*, they certainly do not necessarily agree about *means*, and politics is chiefly about means rather than ends. Second, for reasons which will be discussed when we look at Natural Law, Catholic social doctrine is based upon reason rather than upon revelation, so Catholics claim, and because it is based on reason it is available to all and applicable to all. That is to say,

Catholic proposals in the social sphere are not specifically Catholic. That, at least, is the theory.

Christianity has always had a social agenda: after all, issues of wealth and poverty, violence and injustice occur in the New Testament. Theologians have long debated questions about justice – how one might arrive at a 'just price' – so something on sale in a market was an important topic in the middle ages, and the issue of a 'just wage' was also touched upon. Then, in the sixteenth century with the Spanish and Portugese conquest of the Americas, theologians argued about the rights and wrongs of colonialism. All the time, right down to the end of the nineteenth century, there were discussions about usury, which was interpreted not simply as demanding excessive interest payments for loans made, which is now the usual meaning of usury, but the charging of any interest at all. (These notions, it should be said, were developed at a time when a monetary economy was in its infancy.)

But what is usually today referred to as Catholic social teaching began formally with a letter written by Pope Leo XIII in 1891 called *Rerum Novarum* ('Of new things' – though 'new things' meant revolution, which the Pope was against), which is sometimes, and rather romantically, known as 'The Workers' Charter'. This was a vigorous defence of the established order, and condemned socialism because, the Pope claimed, it was inimical to the best interest of the workers. However, the encyclical defended their right of association in pursuit of their interests – though Leo does not talk of trade unions – and their right to a fair wage and reasonable working conditions as far as hours and time off were concerned. Most strikingly it defended the right to private property. This remained a main theme of social teaching down to the present, although the concept of private property, first conceived of as real estate, has been gradually expanded.

Apart from private property, other themes have been the pursuit of the common good as the main purpose of the state, the damage done by the arms race, the need for international institutions to regulate trade between strong countries and their weaker trading partners, the obligations of wealth and the limitations on capitalism. It also urges the participation of all citizens in the State, and in the management of the industries in which they work, together with the encouragement of profit-sharing.

BOX 8.2   PRINCIPLE OF SUBSIDIARY

An important aspect of participation is expressed in the 'principle of subsidiarity' contained in the encyclical *Quadragesimo anno* ('Forty years on'), issued by Pope Pius XI in 1931. He wrote:

> Just as it is gravely wrong to take from individuals what they can accomplish by their own initiative and industry and give it to the community, so it is an injustice and at the same time a grave evil and disturbance of the right order to assign to a greater and higher association what lesser and subordinate organisations can do.

The emphasis on participation by citizens would seem to suggest that the Church has, in the political sphere, embraced democracy as the preferred form of government. But it has done so only belatedly, and with reservations (democracies, after all, are liable to pass laws which in the eyes of the Church are immoral). The documents always insist that the Church can work with any form of government (except, of course, one which is actively hostile), which is understandable, given that Catholics live in countries with many different kinds of regimes, some of them far removed from democracy. Perhaps more surprising is the rather late commitment to human rights. On the other hand, perhaps this is not surprising: historically the demand for human rights has arisen at the expense of the Church's privileged place in European society. But human rights are notoriously difficult to defend philosophically. The Church's social teaching instead prefers to stress that society itself should be just, rather than put emphasis on the sometimes competing rights of individuals.

This suggests that the Church puts a very positive value on the role of the state. Catholicism, and in this it is distinct from some of the more radical Protestant views, regards the state as necessary for the good of the individual. Its purpose is to guide the interests and activities of citizens towards the common good. This, it proposes, is the natural order of things. State governance is necessary in the natural order: it is not, as some Protestant theorists would argue, the consequence of original sin.

There has been much mention of 'the natural order', so it would perhaps be helpful to say a word at this stage about the style of philosophical thinking which has underlain much of Catholic thinking.

NATURAL LAW

Natural law is sometimes called the *philosphia perennis*, the eternal philosophy. It is not particularly Catholic, or even Christian. One of the best descriptions of it comes from the pagan orator Cicero (Box 8.3).

From a Catholic point of view, the natural law is, as it were, a subset of the divine law, God's law which governs creation. But the natural law is that which we can discover by reason, and which guides our actions. It is allied with the notion, taken from Aristotle – also, obviously, not a Christian – that the end or purpose of human life is contemplation. For Aristotle, that meant philosophical thought; within a Christian context it is contemplation of God. Our lives are ordered to that end. The Greek for end is *'telos'*, so this approach is called teleology. We approach this end by choosing what is good for us, according to the nature of our being – the natural law. We can of course be wrong about what is the truly good; we may be led astray by what seems good on the surface but is ultimately to our detriment; but we cannot be blamed if we make an honest mistake, i.e. if we have followed our consciences.

To use the word 'blame' rather puts this approach into a Christian, or at least a religious, context. But it also applies to a non-religious person in the sense that, by consistently choosing the apparently good over the truly good they will ultimately not achieve happiness. At least, that is the theory!

An example of the natural law in practice is, to take an example from what we have just been talking about, the argument for trade unions. Workers, the argument runs, cannot individually look after themselves. They need to associate with others in order to achieve what is fair for them in their relations with employers. The same is true of the state. The state, natural law philosophers would say, is necessary because without it individuals cannot achieve a properly human mode of existence, as the medieval philosopher and theologian Thomas Aquinas pointed out at the very beginning of his book on government, *De regimine principum* ('On the government of princes' see Box 8.4).

BOX 8.3   NATURAL LAW

There is indeed a true law – right reason – that is in harmony with Nature and present in all things, unchanging and eternal, and that guides us to our duty by its commands and deflects us from wrong-doing by its prohibitions. Its commands and prohibitions never fail to prevail with the good but they have no power to influence the wicked. It is not right to legislate against the requirements of this law and it is not permitted to limit its application. It is impossible for it to be repealed in its entirety and we cannot be exempted from this law even by the Roman people or by the Senate. We do not need to seek out a Sextus Aelius to interpret or expound this law, nor will there be one law in Rome, another in Athens, one law at one time and a different one some time later. One eternal and unchanging law will govern all peoples at all times and it will be, as it were, the single ruling and commanding god of the whole human race. That god is the creator of the law, its proclaimer and its enforcer. The man who does not obey this law is denying his own nature, and, by rejecting his human nature, he will incur the greatest of punishments, even though he will have evaded the other things that are thought of as penalties.

Cicero, *De republica* III xxii

BOX 8.4   NATURAL LAW AND THE STATE

When we consider all that is necessary to human life, it becomes clear that man is naturally a social and political animal, destined more than all other animals to live in community ... One man alone would not be able to furnish himself with all that is necessary, for no one man's resources are adequate to the fullness of human life. For this reason the companionship of his fellows is naturally necessary to man ...

Thomas Aquinas, *De regimine principum*

These, of course, are very general principles. Next we will look at a few particular instances where these general principles have been applied.

THE JUST WAR

A reader of the New Testament might have the impression that Jesus was opposed to the use of violence and therefore that the Church ought likewise to be opposed, and there are indeed a good many Christian pacifists. However, the attitude of Christians to warfare is a complicated story, and it is clear that from early on in the history of the Church, in the time of the Roman Empire, there had been Christians in the imperial army. Some Christians clearly thought that their faith was contrary to all warfare, while others equally clearly thought otherwise.

A theory was developed to permit Christians to go to war in certain circumstances. The conditions for a just war were worked out, but not systematically, by St Augustine in the early fifth century, and then summarised by Aquinas in the thirteenth. They were as follows: first, only the lawful authority may declare war, so a private individual cannot do so; second, there must be a just cause, namely to punish wrongdoing or regain what has been unjustly taken; third, those who declare war must do so for the right intention, namely to secure peace and to punish evildoers. In the sixteenth-century context of the conquest of the Americas a fourth condition was added, that of 'proportionality': the good achieved by the war must be expected to outweigh the damage caused by it.

These principles are open to widely differing interpretations in different situations. Who, for example, does not think his or her own cause 'just'? The question of proportionality can give rise to all sorts of arguments about the impact and effectiveness of different sorts of weapons, or rule certain targets to be illegitimate – this last was a concern which considerably preoccupied the US bishops when they brought out in the 1980s their letter *The Challenge of Peace*. Then there is the issue of who, or what, nowadays constitutes a 'legitimate authority' with the right to declare war, especially when there are international organisations whose task it is to resolve conflicts as far as possible without the taking up of arms. And those involved in peace movements make the point that the very existence of a doctrine of a 'just war' legitimises the use of force. Though the principles may be clear enough, in other words, the application is anything but.

MIGRANTS

The same is true of migrant labourers. Though people who comment on Catholic social doctrine do not often remark it, the papal letters and other documents frequently mention the right of people to travel to different countries in search of work. This was something which was discussed in particular in relation to the settlement of the Americas by the *conquistadores* in the sixteenth century. From the middle ages the moralists had defended the right of people to travel in order to trade (merchants were even supposed to be protected if war was going on around them, alongside women and children and the clergy). Trade, it was sensibly believed, was necessary for human well-being, therefore there was a natural right to travel. Moreover, people (men, in the context) might need to travel abroad in order to find work so that they might fulfil their natural law obligation to provide for their families. But all this was developed before the days of nation states, and certainly before the invention of social security systems. Still, as Catholic social theorists point out, nations who are all in favour of free trade in goods and in capital are being a little inconsistent in opposing free trade in labour.

WOMEN IN THE CHURCH

Finally we come to one of the more contentious issues in Catholicism: the role of women, both in society and in the Church. Clearly, in society at large, women have come to play a much greater role than they used to. Nowadays discrimination against women because of their gender is in very many cases illegal. The Church, however, still operates in a rather more traditional mode. As we have seen, the family is regarded as the basis both of the Church and of society. Even the most recent documents coming from the Vatican emphasise the importance of women as the centre of family life. While such documents accept that women now play an important role in every aspect of life – political, financial, industrial and so on – there is still a pressure coming from Rome for them to be first and foremost mothers and homemakers. It is not that these messages disparage the role of women. Quite the contrary. But they tend to treat the role of women as complementary to, rather than equal to, the role of men. There is, as it were, a division of function: both functions are important, but they are distinct. Feminist writers, not unnaturally, tend to regard the appeal to complementarity as implying that, in fact, women have a secondary role in society

The Catholic Church is, of course, controlled by an all-male priesthood. It is true that the development of religious orders for women allowed many to escape from family ties, and to develop, for instance, leadership skills or other talents which, in the past in the traditional family, they might have found difficulty in so doing. It is nevertheless the case that women are not allowed to be priests in the Roman Catholic Church and, like the laity in general, are ultimately obliged to play a subordinate role. Unlike the rule about celibacy, the prohibition on women priests is claimed to be a matter of doctrine: it is simply not possible, says Rome, to ordain a woman to the priesthood. Should anyone attempt to do so, the argument goes, it would not simply be illegal, it would also be invalid. The ceremony of ordination would make no difference to their status.

Unlike the position of women in the home, which is presented as a natural law argument, the argument against women's ordination is a theological one. First of all, it has never been done – the argument from tradition. Second, Christ chose only men to be his apostles. Third, the priest stands in front of his congregation in the person of Christ, presiding over the Eucharist. It would be inappropriate, so the argument runs, for the person of Christ to be represented by a woman.

These arguments give rise to a whole series of questions, but in essence they come down to one central issue: how far Christian, and not just Catholic, doctrine is culturally conditioned. How far, in this instance, the existence of an exclusively male priesthood is the result of social, historical and even economic factors, rather than theological ones. The question is one which applies much more widely than the problem of whether or not to ordain women to the priesthood. And it is an issue which applies to all brands of Christianity and not just to Catholicism. Deciding which aspects of belief, which demands of morality, can be adapted to modern culture is perhaps the major challenge now confronting the Christian Churches.

So finally in this chapter we turn to the example of an attempt by some theologians to develop an understanding of the Church and its mission which arises directly out of the social and political situation of a particular region of the world. It is called Liberation Theology.

LIBERATION THEOLOGY

It may seem a little strange, after discussing the Catholic Church's social teaching, to return to theology. But one of the problems for the Church, as for many Christian Churches, is that Church members rather compartmentalise their religion. Christianity is for Sunday mass-going, they seem to think, not for the whole of life, whether business or pleasure. The social teaching, in such a context, does not have a major impact on their behaviour.

At a synod in Rome in 1971, however, the bishops who were gathered there to discuss justice in the world produced a document that contained the following remark:

> Action on behalf of justice and participation in the transformation of the world fully appear to us as a constitutive dimension of the preaching of the gospel, or, in other words, of the Church's mission for the redemption of the human race and its liberation from every oppressive situation …

The proposition here spelled out was then incorporated into the Church's canon law, obliging clergy to preach on social issues. This development was undoubtedly brought about by the impact of Liberation Theology which came chiefly, if not only, from Latin America.

Liberation Theology arose in the mid-1960s as a response to the situation of deprivation in which many of the people of those countries to the south of the United States were forced to live. To put it simply, in the past theologians had reflected on the Gospel in the light of their experience of the Church. Liberation Theology reflected upon the Gospel in the light of the experience of the people to whom the Gospel was preached. This meant that the social and political context had to be analysed. Many of the Liberation Theologians turned for this purpose to the analytical tools provided in Marxism, which led to a clash with the authorities in the Vatican who, not unreasonably, regarded Marxism itself as an atheistic doctrine. In Latin America, however, the theologians argued that they were using the tools of Marxism, not its philosophy – though in truth elements of Marxist philosophy certainly occur in their writings.

A further problem that the Vatican had was the emphasis on the 'popular', or people's, Church. The difficulty was that which we have already seen when talking about Basic Christian Communities (see p. 72), which were themselves a manifestation of one aspect of Liberation Theology. This seemed to put the 'popular' Church at odds with the 'official' Church, something which the theologians in Latin America certainly did not intend. They simply meant that they took seriously the popular religion of those countries, one which is much more communal and a good deal less individualistic than the devotional life in Europe described in the previous chapter, and that they built on that.

And there is a deeper issue. Theologians in the Catholic Church are accustomed to thinking of the Church's doctrines as being formulated in, or conditioned by, particular philosophic or theological approaches. The challenge raised by Liberation Theology – and to some extent this does indeed arise from Marxism – is to suggest that these doctrines have been also conditioned by social and economic factors. Liberation Theologians have produced studies which re-examine traditional doctrines from the point of view of the oppressed in Latin America.

Despite the Vatican's hesitations on certain aspects of Liberation Theology, the Church as a whole has begun to embrace the 'option for the poor' which lies at the heart of this new approach. Liberation Theology attempts to integrate the social teaching of the Church and its theology, and to recast them both in a form which reflects the culture of those to whom the Gospel is being preached.

SUMMARY

This chapter has looked at the Church in its relation to the world.

1   The family is 'the building block' of society, a small community, united in faith.

2   The 'pro-life' stance of the Church entails a rejection of contraception – though this teaching is widely ignored, and often challenged – and an opposition to abortion and euthanasia, on which there is less disagreement among Catholics.

3   Politics is a more controversial issue, because some Catholics ('integrists') have attempted in the past to impose a Catholic morality on a confessional state – an attitude now rejected by the Catholic Church.

4   The Church teaches that the state is natural to humanity, not something which arose as a result of Original Sin, and has a positive attitude towards it.

5   The Natural Law is the philosophical theory which has underpinned much of the reflection on the Church and society, as it has been expressed in Catholic social doctrine.

6   Catholic social doctrine began in its modern form in 1891 and has been up-dated by a series of documents ever since. It covers a variety of topics, including:
   a   trade unions, for which support was given from the beginning;
   b   just war, a theory about the rights and wrongs of using military force;
   c   the rights of migrant labour;
   d   women in society.

7   Liberation Theology, the development of theological thinking from the point of view of the oppressed and marginalised, is an attempt to integrate social thinking with theology, and to develop them both in the specific context of a particular place and time.

FURTHER READING

On morality in general, including conscience:

The *Catechism*, pp. 395–9, 426–31, 475–512, 525–37.

McBrien, *Catholicism*, pp. 959–77, 981–1000.

O'Collins, *Catholicism*, pp. 343–58, 361–6.

On Catholic social teaching:

The *Catechism*, pp. 513–24.

McBrien, *Catholicism*, pp. 912–16, 1000–11.

O'Collins, *Catholicism*, pp. 335–43, 358–61.

On Liberation Theology:

Assmann, *Practical Theology of Liberation*, pp. 43–124.

Rowland, *Radical Christianity*, pp. 115–49.

On women's ministry:

Rademacher, *Lay Ministry*, pp. 145–68.

APPENDIX

HISTORY OF THE PAPACY

TO GREGORY THE GREAT

We have seen that there are very early lists of succession to the bishopric of Rome. The great problem with these lists is their highly suspicious regularity. According to them, for most of the first two centuries there seems to have been a new Pope every decade. But is this a 'reading back' of what came to be the case? In fact it is highly unlikely there was a 'bishop' of Rome at all, as the term came to be understood, for the first 150 years. There are two reasons for saying this. First, the relatively late origin of the office of bishop, which was discussed above (see pp. 53, 60). Second, it seems unlikely that there was a single 'bishop' in Rome until about the middle of the second century. It is evident that there was a number of different Christian groups, or communities, representing diverse immigrant populations, which each had their own particular traditions. We know this to have been the case because, during the time of Anicetus ('pope' from 155 to 166, according to the accepted dating), Polycarp, the Bishop of Smyrna, came to visit to discuss the date of Easter: immigrants from Asia Minor had wanted to celebrate it on a special day while Anicetus and his group appeared to be saying that Easter, the day Jesus rose from the dead, was celebrated every Sunday and they did not need a special day.

So by the time of Anicetus there was probably a single individual who had some sort of religious authority over the Christians in Rome, a person of sufficient eminence in the community that Polycarp would come all the way from Asia Minor to speak to him. Before his time, the various groups had been distinct, and probably governed by councils of 'elders'. Rome, of course, was a special case: as the capital of the Roman Empire there were all sorts of different ethnic groups represented among its inhabitants. Hence the emergence of a single 'bishop' was slower here than elsewhere in Christian communities of the Roman world. When a single bishop eventually did emerge, the office holder had a fairly high profile in the city, and was in especial danger when the Christians were being persecuted, as they were from time to time.

PERSECUTION AND ITS AFTERMATH

Persecution was, however, spasmodic, and the Church of Rome was able to consolidate. Under Bishop Fabian (236–50) for instance the city was divided into seven administrative districts for Church purposes, each district in the charge of a cleric known as a deacon. The deacon had particular concern for the social well-being of the Christians, and thus became well-known in the community. For several centuries deacons were to be elected more often than priests to the office of bishop of the city.

One of the problems that bishops had to face was dealing with those who had renounced Christianity during times of persecution. There was a considerable dispute in Rome and in other Churches about how severe one had to be when these renegades ('apostates', in the technical language) wanted to return to the Church. It was clear in the course of this debate in the middle of the third century that Rome had a pre-eminent position and was being consulted on the issue. One of the Bishops most deeply involved was Cyprian, Bishop of Carthage in Africa. He wrote a book on the unity of the Church which gave an especial place to the Bishop of Rome as the centre of this unity. (When the Bishop of Rome's attitude became more sympathetic to those who had lapsed from the faith, Cyprian appears to have rewritten his text to play down the role of Rome.) It was during this debate that Stephen (254–57) applied to his office the text from Matthew, quoted on p. 51. As far as we know he was the first Bishop of Rome to do so.

PROBLEMS WITH EMPERORS

In 313 peace came to the Church with the conversion to Christianity of the Emperor Constantine – though Constantine did not receive baptism until shortly before his death in 337. The Church was endowed with considerable privileges. The bishops were allowed to use the imperial transport system, so that ecumenical councils became possible to resolve the disputes which afflicted Christianity. The Pope of the day did not attend these gatherings, but was represented at them. Relationships with Emperors varied, frequently because Emperors were, in the eyes of the Bishop of Rome, either full-blown heretics or verging on heresy. Matters were complicated because Constantine had founded a new capital city on the site of Greek Byzantium, and called it Constantinople (now Istanbul). The Empire slowly split in two, religiously as well as politically, and the Pope in Rome also found himself at odds with the Patriarch (the chief bishop) of Constantinople.

The Patriarch was much more dominated by the Emperor in Constantinople than the Pope was by the (co-)Emperor in Rome, not least because Rome ceased to the residence of the Emperor in the West, and in any case the office of Emperor was taken over towards the end of the fourth century by rulers of German ancestry, the 'barbarians' whom Rome had originally hired as soldiers. But even the barbarians gave up the title: the last 'Roman' Emperor died before the fifth century was over.

Still, relations with the Emperors – some of whom were, in papal eyes, of doubtful orthodoxy – took up much of a pope's time and energy. There had to be some theory about the relationship between Pope and Emperor. The Emperor Zeno was a particular problem to Pope Gelasius I (492–6). Gelasius wrote him a letter in which he contrasted imperial *power* with papal *authority*, leaving the Emperor in no doubt that the latter was more important: '... you must bend a submissive head to the ministers of divine things', he told Zeno.

Though it varied from time to time, imperial power in Rome in the fifth and sixth centuries was on the whole fairly tenuous, and though for some of the time there was an imperial official in Ravenna supposedly keeping an eye on things on the Emperor's behalf, the bishops of Rome came increasingly to exercise civil authority over their city. They had early started to copy imperial ways – Siricius (384–99), for instance, issued instructions in answer to queries from bishops, rather as emperors issued instructions. Such 'decretals', as they came to be known, were an early part of the Church's canon law. Gregory I (590–604), one of the only two popes to be called 'the Great', had been governor (or 'Prefect') of Rome before becoming a monk, and taking over the civil administration came naturally to him as it collapsed when faced with yet another barbarian onslaught, this time by the Lombards. In particular he reorganised the estates belonging to the papacy in order more efficiently to produce food for the population of his city. It was, incidentally, Pope Gregory who sent missionaries to England, leading eventually to the conversion of Anglo-Saxons to Christianity.

FROM GREGORY I TO INNOCENT III

In the century after the first Gregory, devotion to his memory in England became increasingly widespread. Anglo-Saxon kings sometimes resigned their thrones and made a pilgrimage to Rome to end their days in the city. Popes remained more or less loyal to the Emperor in Constantinople, but that loyalty was frequently stretched, in particular by the 'iconoclast' controversy, when the Emperor Leo (717–41) forbade veneration being given to images (icons). The influence of the Bishop of Rome in the East went into decline, and his power – and the papal estates – were again threatened in the West by the Lombards. As a counter-balance Pope Zachary (741–52) established good relations with the Franks who inhabited a territory roughly equivalent to modern France and part of Germany. They undertook to come to the aid of Zachary's successors when they were under threat, which they did. But not only did the Frankish King Pepin defend the papacy against the Lombards, in 754 he also guaranteed the pope the ownership of great tracts of Italy, despite protests from the Emperor in Constantinople that these lands rightfully belonged to him. This 'donation of Pepin' as it has been called is the origin of the great swathes of Italy which – though precise boundaries frequently changed – survived as the 'papal states' right down to the mid-nineteenth century.

THE FRANKS

The alliance between the papacy and the Franks was formalised when, on Christmas Day 800 Pope Leo III (795–816) crowned Pepin's son, the Frankish ruler Charles the Great (Charlemagne), as Emperor in the West, thus constituting what came to be known as the Holy Roman Empire. What Leo wanted was the protection of the Franks, but in a sense the coronation of Charlemagne sealed an alliance of pope and emperor which was to last for centuries, though not always harmoniously. The Roman Church had been largely instrumental, directly or indirectly, in the conversion of barbarian Europe, thus extending its influence right across the West. In this it was (usually) supported by the Frankish rulers, who appreciated the civilising mission of the Church. There were conflicts, but a strong-minded pope, such as Nicholas I (858–67), could face down a Frankish King, and if need be depose disobedient bishops, even those who enjoyed the support of the King.

The pontificate of Nicholas was the early medieval high point of papal power and prestige. But the authority he had wielded did not long survive him. His successors were weak, and sometimes very immoral. Outside Rome they were threatened by Muslims (known as 'Saracens') invading from North Africa, often via bases in Southern Italy. Inside the city the now lucrative office of pope was fought over by the leading families of Rome. Not that all the popes of the period were weak. John VIII (872–82) led a naval squadron into successful battle against the Saracens, improved Rome's fortifications, and bred horses for his cavalry, as well as attending to his ecclesiastical duties. He was eventually assassinated – beaten to death with a hammer after an attempt to poison him had failed. There were other active Popes, but they were the exception. Such were the problems in Rome that the Frankish rulers no longer sought the title of Roman Emperor: Pope Stephen VI (885–91) bestowed the honour on a nearby duke, the duke of Spoleto, thus surrendering the Pope's independence of local political factions.

DECLINE AND REFORM

The papacy declined into its worst period, even though the pontiffs continued to issue decretals from time to time, and to grant privileges to bishops and monasteries. One of the most immoral was John XII (955–63), who became Pope when only 18 at the wishes of his father. He was naturally more interested in women and hunting than in ecclesiastical ceremonial, but was faced by an attack from the King of Italy who was trying to take over Rome. John appealed for help to Otto, King of the Saxons, who came to Rome and was crowned Emperor after capturing most of Northern Italy. Emperor Otto, however, deposed John for immorality, and required the Romans not to choose another Pope without imperial consent. This was of course not at all what John had intended, and he tried to make a comeback when Otto had left the city, but seems to have been murdered (there are differing accounts of his death, all of them lurid). But with the arrival of the Ottonian dynasty the slow journey of the papacy back to respectability and international influence began.

The journey gathered momentum under Otto III, who appointed first a German and then a Frenchman to the office of Pope. This was at the beginning of the eleventh century. By the middle of the century the papal entourage included clerics from all over Europe, and Pope Leo IX (1049–55) was declared by a Council in Rheims to be the 'Universal Primate'. It was during his period of office, in 1054, that Rome and Constantinople finally and formally split apart, and developed into two separate Churches. The reforms which Leo and his successors put in place are sometimes known as the 'Gregorian reforms' because they are especially associated with Pope Gregory VII (1073–85: Gregory was called Hildebrand before his election, and the reforms are sometimes known as the Hildebrandine reforms). The reformers had a number of aims: to improve the morality of the clergy and to enforce celibacy; to outlaw the practice of buying one's way into ecclesiastical office (a sin called simony); and to free the Church from the control of lay magnates. This last is known as the 'investiture contest', because the sign of a magnate's authority over a bishop was his right to hand him – invest him with – the symbols of his office. The conflict between the popes and the powerful laity of Europe over this issue lasted 50 years. The popes eventually won, though magnates continued to exercise some control over appointments to bishoprics for generations to come.

By common consent, the most powerful and effective pope of the high middle ages was Innocent III (1198–1216). He made and unmade kings. He held a major council of the Church to reform the lives of the clergy as well as Church structures. He thought, with the capture of Constantinople by 'crusaders' who theoretically were on their way to Palestine to free the Holy Land from the control of Muslims, that he had re-united the Church of Constantinople with that of Rome. He improved the finances of the papacy and streamlined its bureaucracy. Under his pontificate Rome was increasingly approached by bishops from the Christian world who sought his adjudication when matters were in dispute. In place of the title of 'vicar of St Peter', which had been commonly used for centuries, Innocent III applied to himself the grander title of 'Vicar of Christ': it encapsulated the wide range of papal claims to what had come to be called the 'plenitude of power' (*plenitudo potestatis*).

FROM INNOCENT III TO CLEMENT VII

The power which the popes now claimed was ultimately self-destructive. The papacy with its vast estates and political clout was an office many senior churchmen coveted. It was fought over at elections by representatives of the great families, especially of Italy. The elections were frequently long-drawn-out, and conclaves were invented to try to speed up the process of choosing a pope. On one occasion, so great were the divisions among the electors that they chose a simple hermit, Pietro da Morrone, as Celestine V. It was a disaster, and he resigned after only a few months (July to December 1294). His successor, Boniface VIII (1294–1303) had grandiose ambitions which culminated in an encyclical called *Unam Sanctam* ('One holy', 1302) which claimed that outside the authority of the pope there was no forgiveness of sin, no hope of salvation. The traditional Latin phrase *extra ecclesiam nulla salus* – 'outside the Church there is no salvation' – was taken a stage further to bolster papal pretensions. Those pretensions were put to the test in a confrontation between Boniface and the King of France – and the Pope lost. The power over monarchs which Innocent had exercised a century earlier had all but disappeared.

THE AVIGNON PAPACY

This was vividly demonstrated by the decision of Clement V (1305–14) to settle in Avignon. It was impracticable for him to return to Rome, which was in the hands of one of the Pope's enemies (he had been elected in Perugia and crowned in Lyons), so he set up his court in a town which was, strictly speaking, a dependency of the Kingdom of Naples. It was surrounded by papal lands and the popes eventually bought the town of Avignon itself from Naples. So it was not formally French, but lay close to French dominions. A series of French popes, culminating in Gregory XI (1370–8), remained in Avignon in what became known as the 'Babylonian captivity'. Gregory, however, moved his court back to Rome in 1377, establishing his official residence in the Vatican palace besides St Peter's basilica (hitherto it had been in the Lateran palace beside the basilica of St John Lateran, which was, and remains, the Bishop of Rome's own cathedral).

THE GREAT SCHISM

The election which followed Gregory's death was particularly difficult, especially because the Roman mob laid siege to the electors, fearing they would choose someone who would move the papal court out of Rome once more. Urban VI (1378–89) immediately showed himself a very abrasive individual, perhaps even psychologically unbalanced. Many of the electors, the French leading the way, expressed regret at their choice, argued that they had not made their choice freely, and went on to elect a rival pope. This began the 'Great Western Schism', when there were two popes (three after the 1409 Council of Pisa tried to settle the dispute by choosing yet a third candidate). The schism was settled at the Council of Constance, when one pope resigned and the other two were deposed. Odo Colonna, a member of one of the great Roman families which had long fought over control of the papacy, became Martin V (1417–31).

There were, among the popes of the fifteenth century, a number of admirable men, but the schism had almost destroyed the prestige of the office, and the officer-holders themselves were frequently more concerned about advancing the fortunes of their families than governing the Church. Perhaps the nadir of the papacy in the second millennium was the pontificate of Alexander VI, the Spaniard Rodrigo Borgia or Borja (1492–1503). Alexander was concerned above all to advance his family, and he had ten illegitimate children by several mistresses, to many of whom – both mistresses and children – he was deeply devoted. The extravagant and profligate life he lived before his election did not stop after it, but despite his immorality and dedication to the acquisition of wealth he emerged as a considerable figure on the world stage. He it was who was asked to divide the new-found Americas into spheres of influence of the Spanish and Portugese.

THE REFORMATION

Julius II (1503–13) was Alexander's successor but one – the intervening pope ruling only a matter of months. Julius may have been more at home on the battlefield than at the altar, but he was also a considerable patron of the arts and began the demolition of the medieval basilica of St Peter's and its reconstruction as the magnificent baroque church which exists today. It took more than a century to complete, and at the start it was paid for partly by the sale of indulgences across Europe. In Germany this profanation of holy things – eventually combined with other doubts about Roman Catholic theological positions – gave rise to Martin Luther's revolt against the Church and the establishment of an alternative Christian system which came to be called Protestantism.

It fell to Leo X (1513–21) to deal with Luther's revolt, but he had little interest in the reform of the Church for which Luther was calling. He was more concerned with enjoying the papacy ('God has given us the papacy, let us enjoy it', he is reputed to have said), hunting, carnivals and his patronage of the arts. The papacy fell ever more deeply into debt, and the electors chose an ascetic cardinal from Utrecht as Hadrian VI (1522–23). Hadrian was in Spain at the time of his election. He was very close to the Emperor Charles V, whose tutor he had been. He did not survive long enough to undertake significant reforms of the Church, and Hadrian's successor, Clement VII

(1523–34), was more interested in the arts than in the situation in Germany. Clement had been elected for his supposed political skills, but they proved not to be up to the admittedly difficult tasks which faced him. In the end German troops, many of them followers of Luther, sacked Rome in 1527. Clement was now at the mercy of the Emperor, who happened to be the nephew of Catherine of Aragón whom the English King Henry VIII wished to divorce. Given the power of the Emperor, Clement was never in a position to grant this – and the Church in England went into schism from Rome.

FROM CLEMENT VII TO JOHN PAUL II

Clement, dependent upon the goodwill of the Emperor, was forced to bow to his wishes and agree to a reforming Council of the Church. Charles V was concerned that his German dominions in particular were divided between Catholics and Protestants, and he wanted a united faith to heal the divisions which had emerged. The Council of Trent was eventually called by Clement's successor Paul III (1534–49), and met in three periods and twenty-five sessions between 1545 and 1562. It failed to reunite the Church, but imposed a great number of reforms on Catholicism in all its aspects – the discipline and education of the clergy, the residence of bishops in their dioceses, a revision of the Church's administrative structure. It also reaffirmed Catholic doctrine, revised the liturgy, brought out a catechism of the Catholic faith and imposed numerous other changes on a not altogether willing Church. Countries, France in particular, which thought they had in the past done things in their own way, resented the centralising of power in Rome. But Trent nevertheless breathed new vitality into the Church and reinspired the new missionary movement which had begun with the discovery of the New World at the end of the fifteenth century. Not all the popes who were to follow could be included in the ranks of the great and the good, but none ever again descended to the level of an Alexander VI, and not a few were very holy men.

THE PROBLEM OF THE JESUITS

The part that popes played in the politics of Europe decreased as the centuries went by. The papal states still existed, but the papal army, which at the beginning of the seventeenth century had numbered some 50,000 men, by the end of the eighteenth was down to about 3,000. Their role was mainly to act as a police force. The papacy was concerned mainly with internal problems of the Church, including some to which the religious order called the Jesuits gave rise. The Jesuits had been founded in the 1530s, receiving their papal 'charter' in 1540. The Society of Jesus, to give it the full name, was the Church's major missionary arm, as well as the educator of the children of the elite classes of Europe. It also produced some of the most significant theologians. There were rather esoteric clashes over Jesuit theology; more importantly, the Jesuit attempt to adapt the liturgy of the Catholic Church to the culture of the Chinese was met with hostility by other missionaries in China, and was ultimately banned by the papacy in what became known as the 'Chinese rites' controversy. In 1700 the Chinese Emperor himself wrote to Pope Innocent XII in defence of the Jesuits, but to no avail.

As the eighteenth century went on, however, a much greater threat to the Jesuits appeared. Governments across Europe became hostile. They were expelled from Portugal, France and Spain, and the courts of France and Spain demanded of Clement XIII (1758–69) that he entirely suppress the Jesuits. This he refused to do, but his successor Clement XIV (1769–74) issued an order, a 'Bull', suppressing the Society in 1773. Some across Europe saw this act as the first step on the way to getting rid of the papacy itself. As the nation states developed, the existence of a supranational power such as the papacy was troublesome to politicians. Even those who were not actively hostile to the papacy as such wanted the Church in their own countries brought more closely under state control, to the disadvantage of the papacy.

When the French Revolution broke out Pope Pius VI's (1775–99) problems increased a hundredfold. It seemed that, with the Church in France officially brought under state control, the papal states destroyed by Napoleon's armies, and the Pope himself bundled off as a captive to France where he died, prophecies that the papacy's days were numbered seemed to be coming true. Pius VII (1800–23) was elected in Venice, but returned to Rome. He was summoned to Paris by Napoleon to crown him as Emperor (the last 'Holy Roman Emperor', the Austrian Emperor, resigned the title in 1806), but in 1809 was seized and carried off to captivity in France just as his predecessor had been. He was, however, released even before Napoleon was defeated, and returned to Rome in 1814 something of a hero to devout Catholics. One of Pius's first acts on his return was to re-establish the Society of Jesus.

A REINVIGORATED PAPACY

At the peace conference of 1815 to end the Napoleonic wars (the Congress of Vienna) the papal states were restored. Successive popes attempted to re-establish their authority there, but could only do so by draconian police measures. Pius IX (1846–79) was elected in the belief that he would be more liberal in his ideas than his immediate predecessors, but that proved not to be the case. As Italy was gradually unified, the papal states disappeared, until only Rome itself was left. That fell to the Italians in 1870 when the French troops guarding it were withdrawn.

The Pope's conservatism was expressed in 1864 in what was known as the 'Syllabus of Errors', a list of propositions condemning various philosophical theories, but also liberalism and socialism. The final condemnation (number 80) insisted that it was wrong to believe that the pope could, or even ought to, come to terms with modern civilisation. In 1870 the First Vatican Council declared that the Pope was infallible and exercised primacy over the whole Church (see pp. 58ff.) These decrees, bolstering the papacy after the loss of the papal states, helped to centralise authority in the Vatican, a process which had gained momentum with growing ease of travel and communication, and with the revival of the missionary enterprise which was firmly Rome-based. Increasingly, too, episcopal appointments were drawn from clergy who had been educated at the Roman colleges and were familiar with the Vatican system. Pius IX declared himself, after the loss of the papal states, a 'prisoner in the Vatican'. There was a wave of sympathy throughout the Catholic world, which also strengthened papal pretensions.

Although the Kingdom of Italy had promptly offered to resolve the isolation of the papacy by recognising its independence and compensating it for the loss of its territories, it was not until 1929 and the 'Lateran accords' that a solution was found. The papacy was indeed compensated – though not indeed as much as it might have been, Italy itself being short of funds at the time – and an independent, sovereign state, the world's smallest by far, was set up as the Vatican City State with the pope as a temporal sovereign, thus theoretically guaranteeing his independence.

This independence was put to the test during the Second World War, but belligerents on both sides respected it. The pope of the day, Pius XII (1939–58), attempted to observe strict neutrality. There is certainly evidence that, though he was a Germanophile, he favoured the Allied, as distinct from the Axis, powers, but he was to come under much criticism for failing to condemn the genocide wrought upon the Jews by the Nazis. That he did not do so is evident; why he did not do so is much less clear, and there is no simple explanation.

REFORM OF THE CHURCH

After the war Pius XII saw his role to be, as someone unkindly put it, a 'Vatican oracle', speaking out on an enormous range of issues. His successor, John XXIII (1958–63), was a very different character. He saw it as his task to help the Church to come to terms with the modern world – the very notion which Pius IX had condemned in the Syllabus of Errors. For this purpose he summoned the Second Vatican Council (1962–65) whose deliberations, expressed in a range of documents from a study of the Church itself to reflections on modern means of communication, made an enormous impact not just on Catholicism but on very many Christian denominations.

In the course of his pontificate John became a much-loved character, and is credited with beginning the process not just of 'updating' the Church, but of improving relations with the Communist countries, including the Soviet Union. Paul VI (1963–78), his successor, continued the policy, developing what was called the 'Ostpolitik', or 'Eastern policy', of detente. Paul was in turn followed by John Paul I, who died after only a month in office, and John Paul I by John Paul II, a Pole, and the first non-Italian since Hadrian VI was elected in 1522. His triumphant return to Poland in 1979 (the first of several such visits), his understanding of Communism from the inside and his support of opposition movements in Poland, especially the trade-union-based Solidarity, all contributed to speeding the collapse of the Communist regimes of Eastern Europe, and of Russia itself. His many trips around the world have made the papacy much more immediate both to Catholics and to non-Catholics. It has also contributed to the increased centralisation of authority in Rome, which many in the Catholic Church consider to be a contradiction of what the Second Vatican Council stood for.

SUMMARY

1 The bishopric of Rome (the papacy) developed fairly late, probably not until the mid-second century.

2 From early on, however, it was regarded as having special authority.

3 It rapidly developed a complex administrative structure, both for dealing with Church problems in Western Europe, and for taking care of the people of Rome.

4 The gradual separation of the Eastern Empire from the Western left the papacy vulnerable. As a result, popes had to seek allies among, in particular, the Franks.

5 With some notable exceptions, the popes of the ninth and tenth centuries were not powerful figures, some of them being distinctly decadent.

6 The (future) German Emperor Otto was called upon for help, and he instigated a period of reform.

7 The Church was thus left somewhat at the mercy of feudal barons, and in the 'investiture contest' the pope strove to regain authority.

8 Authority was further damaged, partly by the long residence of the popes in Avignon, but more so by the 'Great Schism' which followed.

9 The Protestant Reformation was sparked by the sale of indulgences, which in turn was occasioned by the need to raise money for the rebuilding of St Peter's in Rome.

10 The Council of Trent was called in a vain attempt to reunite the Church, but it did succeed in reforming Catholic life and reaffirming Catholic doctrine.

11 With the evolution of modern nation states, the papacy became of less significance in European affairs, and was often at the beck and call of the great powers.

    a An example of this was the suppression of the Jesuits.

    b Napoleon twice forcibly removed the pope of the day from Rome to France.

12 In the nineteenth century the papacy recovered much of its prestige, though as a spiritual force rather than as a temporal power.

    a All temporal power was removed in 1870, to be restored in a very modest fashion in 1929 with the establishment of the Vatican City State.

13 The Second Vatican Council made major reforms of the Church, and the reign of John Paul II has made the papacy much better known worldwide.

FURTHER READING

Duffy, *Saints and Sinners.*

Kelly, *Oxford Dictionary of Popes.*

Walsh, *The Conclave.*

GLOSSARY

The list which follows contains technical terms – and some others – which may be unfamiliar to readers of this book. Words within entries which have been emboldened are themselves – or their near relations – entries in the Glossary.

absolution the act of a priest in forgiving sins (i.e. 'absolving' someone from his or her sins)

acolytes originally one of the four **minor orders** with a variety of functions; but now used of those who help at mass, and carry candles during the **liturgy**

ad limina a Latin term meaning literally 'to the threshold', i.e. to the tombs of the **apostles** Peter and Paul; it is used of the five-yearly visits made by **bishops** to the Vatican

apostles the twelve closest followers of Jesus, regarded in **Catholicism** as the precursors of **bishops**; the word comes from the Greek 'to send'

Apostles' Creed a shorter statement of faith than the **Nicene Creed**, one which emerges towards the end of the fourth century, already attributed at that point to the **apostles**

apostolic delegate an emissary of the **pope** who is accredited to the **hierarchy** of the country to which he is sent, rather than to the government

apostolic succession the theory according to which the authority of the **apostles** is handed down to **bishops**

baptism the first of the **sacraments**, a form of ritualised washing, which indicates entry into Christianity

basilica nowadays a large or particularly important church, but originally a particular architectural style of building which was used first for Roman imperial functions and then for churches

beatification the first stage on the way to **canonisation**; someone who is beatified is thereafter known by the title 'Blessed'

bishop the chief priest of a **diocese**; it derives from the Greek 'episcopus' meaning an 'overseer' – hence the adjective 'espiscopal', and the word for bishops as a group, 'episcopate'; see also **episcopalian**

bull a particularly formal papal document, so called from its seal (in Latin, 'bulla')

Canon the word has a variety of meanings; it is used of the central prayer of the **Eucharist**, the canon of the **mass**, of an individual law contained in the **Code of Canon Law**, of the approved list of books of the **Old** and **New Testaments**, and it is also the name of a rank in the **Catholic** priesthood, used of those who priests serve as the advisors to the **bishop** and are attached to his **cathedral**; see also **Vincentian Canon**

Canon Law the formal law of the **Catholic** Church, now contained in the **Code of Canon Law**

canonisation the formal ceremony by which a person renowned for holiness is declared by the **pope** to be a saint; the process by which this comes about is administered by the **Congregation** for the Causes of Saints; someone who is declared a saint may be venerated during the Church's **liturgy**

cardinal highest-ranking **cleric** in the **Catholic** Church after the **pope**; the origin of the term is uncertain, but those called 'cardinals' were originally the bishops of the ancient **sees** around the city of Rome, and the priests in charge of the most important churches of the city; they meet in consistories to discuss matters with the pope (though some of these are purely formal), and in **conclaves** to elect a pope

catechism from the Greek 'to instruct', a way of teaching Christian **doctrine**; in recent tradition, printed catechisms have been in a question-and-answer form

Catechism of the Catholic Church an official, lengthy statement of the (Roman) **Catholic** faith in a series of numbered paragraphs, *not* in question-and-answer form, published in 1992 (English translation 1994); a revised edition came out in in English in 1999

catechumen those subject to catechetical instruction (see **catechism**) while preparing for **baptism**; they were originally allowed to attend only the first part of the **mass**, which was called 'the mass of the catechumens'

cathedral the chief church of a **diocese**, where a **bishop** has his 'cathedra' or seat

Catholic from a Greek term meaning 'universal' or 'worldwide', hence the (Roman) Catholic Church is a worldwide **communion**; but the term is also used in contrast to **Protestant**, and means a particular tradition – for example, the practice of government by **bishops**

celebrant the person, almost always a priest or **bishop**, who presides at the formal **liturgy**

celibacy the requirement, imposed on **Catholic** priests in the Western Church (not always in the Eastern) to remain unmarried; technically it is distinct from **chastity**, but is obviously closely linked to it

chastity the requirement, sometimes imposed by a **vow**, to refrain from all sexual activity

clergy the body of **clerics**

cleric someone in **Holy Orders**, including in **Minor Orders**

clerks regular groups of clerics, usually priests, who live together in community under a **rule**, and engage in active pastoral work; they constitute a **religious order**, but are to be distinguished from **monks** and **friars**

Code of Canon Law the book containing the law of the Church; until the beginning of the twentieth century Church law was contained in many different, and sometimes contradictory, pieces of legislation, which had been issued by **councils**, or by **popes**, or even by individual **bishops**; this was known as the *Corpus Iuris Canonici*, 'the collection of canon law'; at the beginning of the last century it was decided to organise and rationalise the *Corpus Iuris Canonici* into book form, the *Codex Iuris Canonici*. This Code was first published in 1917, and it was again published in a much revised form in 1983. There is a separate Code for the Eastern Churches

collegiality the **doctrine**, endorsed at **Vatican II**, that all the Church's **bishops**, in union with the **pope**, are collectively ('collegially') responsible for the well-being of the Church

communion this word has several interconnected meanings: (1) the group of Churches which share the same beliefs and have some common **hierarchical** structure, are said to be 'in communion' with each other and are described as 'a communion', for example, the Anglican Communion; (2) in some Churches, though not usually the **Catholic** Church, the central act of worship, the **Eucharist**, is called 'the communion service'; (3) the act of receiving the Eucharist is said, particularly among **Catholics**, as 'going to communion'

conciliarism the theory that authority in the Church lies with a **council**

consistory *see* **cardinal**

conclave comes from the Latin *'con clave'*, 'with a key', signifying that the **cardinals** are locked in when they meet to elect a **pope**

concordat the name given to treaties between the **Holy See** and a government

confirmation the **sacrament** which, along with **baptism** and the **Eucharist**, constitute initiation into Christianity

Congregation a word with several meansings: (1) one of the senior departments of the papal **curia**, usually managed by a **cardinal**; (2) the word is also used sometimes of **religious orders**: (3) it is commonly used of the group of people gathered for worship

Congregation for Bishops the **dicastery** in the **Vatican** responsible for the appointment of **bishops**

Congregation for Divine Worship the **dicastery** in the **Vatican** responsible for the Church's **liturgy**

Congregation for Eastern Churches the **dicastery** in the **Vatican** responsible for the Churches of the East which do not have a tradition of a Latin **liturgy**

Congregation for the Causes of Saints *see* **beatification, canonisation**

Congregation for the Clergy the **dicastery** in the **Vatican** responsible for the well-being of the **clergy**

Congregation for the Doctrine of the Faith the **dicastery** in the **Vatican** responsible for the **orthodoxy** of belief

Congregation for the Evangelisation of Peoples the **dicastery** in the **Vatican** responsible for the missionary activity of the Church, and in general for the Church in missionary areas

consubstantiation the theological theory that, in the **mass**, though the bread and wine become the body and blood of Christ, the bread and wine themselves remain alongside the body and blood of Christ

council of the Church a gathering of **bishops** of the Church to decide important matters of faith, or of Church discipline

Council of Basel a **council** of the Church (1431–39), which supported the **conciliarist** convictions of the **Council of Constance**

Council of Constance a **council** of the Church (1414–18), called to resolve the divisions occasioned by the **Great Schism**

Council of Nicaea a **council** of the Church (325), called to settle a dispute about the nature of Christ

Council of the Vatican *see* **Vatican I**, **Vatican II**

Council of Trent a **council** of the Church (1543–63), called to resolve both **doctrinal** and disciplinary matters brought into prominence by the **Reformation**

creed a formal statement of faith; the best-known are the **Apostles' Creed** and the **Nicene Creed**

curia Latin for 'court', it denotes the administration of a **bishop** or, more frequently in modern **Catholic** usage, the administration of the whole Church, located in the **Vatican**

deacon from the Greek for 'servant', a rank of **cleric**, junior to a **priest**, who was responsible for the charitable work in an area, but also had some role in the **liturgy**; it became simply a stage on the way to ordination as a **priest**

decretals papal letters which had the force of **canon law**

deuterocanonical a word for books which are contained in the Greek, but do not occur in the Hebrew, Bible (the **Old Testament**)

dicastery the word used for departments of the **curia**

diocese the administrative unit of the Church, presided over by a **bishop**; it is an area which is regarded as being self-supporting, or at least capable of being self-supporting

Divine Office the recitation of the **psalms**, together with other prayers and readings, which is required of **Catholic** priests and members of **religious orders**; it is the official prayer of the Church; a shortened version, the Little Hours, is said by many **Catholics** as an act of devotion

doctrine from the Latin meaning teaching – what the Church teaches in a general sense

dogma those Christian beliefs which are held to be revealed truths, established beyond doubt and to be held by all

doxology a hymn or prayer of glory (as distinct from a petitionary prayer) to God

ecumenical from a Greek word meaning 'the whole world'; it is used to denote efforts to establish better relations between Churches, in the phrase, for instance, 'the ecumenical movement'; it is used in a rather different sense by **Catholics** in the term **ecumenical council**

ecumenical councils gatherings of bishops representative of the whole (**Catholic**) Church; the decrees of such **councils** are regarded as binding on the whole Church

encyclical a letter which is circulated; originally applied to the letters of any **bishop** which were meant to be distributed among surrounding bishops, but it now restricted to certain important letters from the **pope**

epiclesis the prayer calling down the Holy Spirit upon the bread and wine during the **Eucharist**

episcopal *see* **bishop**

episcopalian the adjective given to those Churches which accept government by **bishops**, as distinct from those which, at least in theory, have government by the **congregation**

episcopate *see* **bishop**

Eucharist from a Greek word meaning 'thanksgiving', the term used both for the service in which the bread and wine become the body and blood of Christ at the consecration, and for the consecrated elements which are received in **communion**

exorcists originally one of the **Minor Orders**, theoretically charged with the driving out of demons, though this – when it happens at all, which is very rarely – is now restricted to senior **clergy**

friar from the Latin *'frater'* for 'brother', a member of a **religious order**, usually engaged in apostolic work, such as preaching; unlike **monks** they move from place to place

heresy serious theological error, or departure from **orthodoxy**

heretical the adjective derived from **heresy**

hierarchy from two Greek words meaning 'the rule of priests' and generally used to denote the structure of authority in the Church (and now, more widely, of the structure of authority in general)

Holy Orders the **sacrament** by means of which someone becomes a **priest** or a **bishop**

Holy See the term used for the juridical existence of the **pope** and the **curia** as a sovereign entity in international law

host in this context, the form of bread, usually in **Catholicism** a round disc, used in the **Eucharist** and received in **communion**

indulgences a means by which, by saying certain prayers or, for instance, by going on pilgrimage, a sinner may mitigate the punishment in the next life for faults committed in this; a plenary indulgence is believed to remove all such punishment

infallibility the belief that the **pope**, when teaching formally to the whole Church about matters of faith or morals, cannot make a mistake; instances of such teaching are rare

integrism a cast of mind that holds everything within **Catholicism** to be equally important; it commonly also embraces the belief that Catholic morality ought to dictate the law of the state, and that only Catholicism can be freely exercised, though other faiths may be tolerated

lector Latin for 'reader', originally one of the **Minor Orders**

litany from the Greek meaning 'petition', a series of (usually short) phrases, to which the **congregation** responds with a standard phrase such as 'pray for us', or 'hear our prayer'

Little Hours *see* **Divine Office**

liturgy from the Greek meaning, literally, 'the work of the people'; it is used in the Christian Churches of public, formal acts of worship

mass the common name for the **Eucharist**, the central religious service of the **Catholic** Church; the name is probably derived from the final words of dismissal of the congregation which occur in the Latin **liturgy** of the mass, '*Ite missa est*'

Minor Orders the offices of doorkeeper or porter, **lector**, **exorcist** and **acolyte**; these have now been abolished as offices to which one is in any sense 'ordained', but they used to be steps on the way to the Major Orders of **deacon**, **priest** and **bishop**

missal the book which contains the **liturgy** of the **mass**

monarchical episcopate the term sometimes used of **bishops** who 'ruled' dioceses, a form of government which is first attested in Asia Minor at the end of the first century AD, and gradually spread throughout the Church; it is thought to have arrived rather late in Rome

monk someone who lives in a monastery according to a **rule**, that is to say lives a stable life in one place rather than travelling around, as do **friars** or **clerks regular**

New Testament the books of **scripture** written, it is thought, from about AD 60 to no later than AD 120, which recount the life of Jesus, and contain letters, attributed to some of Jesus's earliest followers, reflecting upon Jesus's message

Nicene creed a statement of faith, believed to have been drawn up by the **Council of Nicaea**

nun technically, the female equivalent of **monk**, but more generally used of any woman who is a member of a **religious order**

nuncio a papal diplomat with the rank of ambassador, one, that is, who is accredited to a sovereign government

Old Testament the collection of sacred books of the Jewish **scriptures**, sometimes called the Hebrew Bible, which are included with the **New Testament** as part of the Christian scriptures

order *see* **Holy Orders**, **Minor Orders**, **religious order**

ordination the conferring of the **sacrament** of **Holy Orders**, by which someone becomes a **deacon**, **priest** or **bishop**

original sin the sin of Adam and Eve recounted in the **Old Testament**, through which the human race was cut off from God, and which is handed down to the rest of the humanity from Adam and Eve; its effects are reversed by the **redemption**

orthodox/orthodoxy the word means 'correct belief', as distinct from **heresy** or heretical belief, and in that sense is used widely by all Churches; however, the Orthodox Churches are a **communion** (in sense 1 above) of Churches which originated in the Eastern part of the Roman Empire, and are not in communion with the **pope** (it is necessary to say 'originated', because emigration from this area has given rise to Orthodox Churches elsewhere)

penance either the **sacrament** by which sins are forgiven, or a pious practice, such as going on **pilgrimage** or saying certain prayers, to expiate the guilt associated with sin

pilgrimage a journey made, often as an act of **penance**, to a certain place, often the **shrine** of a **saint** or the sites in the Holy Land associated with the life of Jesus; for **Catholics**, Rome is a common destination with its shrines of Sts Peter and Paul

plenary indulgence *see* **indulgences**

pontiff from the Latin *pontifex maximus*, a title used of the pagan chief priest at Rome, for a time held by the Emperor, and gradually transferred to the **pope**

Pontifical Councils the more recently created **dicasteries** of the **curia**

pontifical faculties papally-approved university departments of **Catholic** universities

pontificals although the word **pontiff** refers to the **pope**, the adjective is used of **bishops** in general, and 'pontificals' commonly refers to the formal dress of a bishop

pope the **bishop** of Rome, from the Greek *pappas* meaning 'father'; though originally applied to any **bishop** – indeed, to **priests** as well – from the eighth century in the West it was largely, and from the eleventh century entirely, restricted to the bishop of Rome

prayer turning to God in praise or petition; there are many set formulas of prayers, but prayer can also be reflecting on, for instance, the life of Christ – in which case it is often called meditation

presbyter the word from which **priest** is derived, but originally meaning 'elder', and taken over from the name given to those who ran Jewish synagogues

priest derived from **presbyter**; the idea of priesthood within Christianity developed slowly as the **doctrine** of the **Eucharist** as a **sacrifice** gradually evolved: the priest is the one who offers the sacrifice of the **mass**

primacy from the Latin *primus*, 'first': as defined at **Vatican I** it asserts that the **pope** has authority over the whole **Catholic** Church, though this must be without detriment to the authority of the local **bishop**

Protestantism a term arising from the Diet of Speyer in 1529 when those who had embraced the **Reformation** movement of Luther protested (hence the name) at the attempt by **Catholic** powers to reverse the reformation; nowadays, however, it tends to be used of those Christians who sharply diverge from the Catholic tradition – which paradoxically would not include Lutherans

psalms a collection of 150 hymns in the Hebrew Bible (the **Old Testament**); they are widely used in the Christian **liturgy**, and especially in the **Divine Office**

psalter the collection of **psalms** in a book

redemption the **doctrine** that, through the life and death of Christ, humankind is delivered from the consequences of **original sin**, which separated humanity from God

Reformation in the context of this book, the sixteenth-century movement begun by Martin Luther (1483–1546) which divided Western Christianity and gave rise to **Protestantism**

religious orders organisations of men or women (and very occasionally both together) living a life under **vows** according to a particular **rule**

rite a solemn ceremony of the **liturgy** and, by extension, to all liturgical ceremonies performed in a particular way; for example, in the Western **Catholic** Church the liturgy used to be, and occasionally still is, celebrated in Latin, so this is the 'Latin rite' of the **Catholic** Church; there are other rites within the Catholic Church, and of course outside it

rubrics the instructions contained in **missals** and other books about how the **liturgy** is to be performed, so called because these instructions were written in red (*'ruber'* in Latin)

rule in the context of this book, a guide to a particular form of living, usually under **vows**, and often drawn up by the founder of a **religious order**

sacrament a visible sign of the presence of Christ, brought about through a **liturgical** action

Sacred Heart a devotion to the love of Christ, symbolised by depictions of Christ with a heart visible on his chest

sacrifice a ceremony carried out by a **priest** which typically involved the slaying of a victim, and offering the victim to God, an idea which is common to many religions; in Christianity, Christ's death is seen as a sacrifice which, in **Catholic** thought, is re-presented in the **Eucharist**

saint someone whose holiness of life has led the Church to approve him or her as a person who may be publicly venerated

scriptures the word comes from Latin and simply means 'writings', but as a term is used of the sacred writings of many religions; in

Christianity the scriptures comprise both the **Old** and the **New Testaments**

see the equivalent of **diocese**, from the latin '*sedes*' ('seat'), where a **bishop** has his seat

shrine originally the place where the bones of a **saint** were thought to be, though the word has been extended to include other sites which for one reason or another are deemed to be holy

synod a gathering of **bishops** (usually) for a meeting; in current (Roman) **Catholic** usage it differs from a **council** because its authority is less

tabernacle from the Latin for 'tent', the small chest in which the **hosts** are retained after they have been consecrated during the **Eucharist**

teleology from the Greek word for 'end', hence a theory that existence has an end or purpose

terna the list of three names sent, usually by the **nuncio** or other papal representative, to Rome when a new **bishop** needs to be chosen

transubstantiation the doctrine that, during the **Eucharist**, the bread and wine are completely transformed into the body and blood of Christ, and that the appearance of bread and wine which remain is precisely that, an appearance only

Vatican used variously of the papal palace in Rome, the papal **curia**, the authority of the **pope**; it is the name of the hill on which St Peter's basilica was built in the fourth century, probably over the grave of St Peter himself

Vatican City State created in 1929 by an agreement between the **Holy See** and the (then) Kingdom of Italy to provide a neutral country of residence for the **pope**; it is the world's smallest state and lies almost wholly within Rome, situated around the **Vatican** palace and St Peter's **basilica**

Vatican I a council of the Church (1869–70) which defined the pope's primacy and infallibility

Vatican II a council of the Church (1962–65) which reformulated much of the **Catholic** Church's thinking on issues such as the Church itself, the **liturgy**, the Church's relationship to the world, and much else; it propounded the **doctrine** of **collegiality**

vernacular the current, modern language; in Roman **Catholicism** normally contrasted with the Latin language which until the 1960s was used in the Western Church for the **liturgy**

vestments the formal dress worn by **celebrants** during the **liturgy**

Vincentian canon named after Vincent of Lérins – an island in the Mediterranean near Cannes – who died in about the year AD 450; he formulated a test to distinguish **heresy** from **orthodoxy**, arguing what what was orthodox had been believed everywhere, always and by everybody

vows solemn promises, in Roman **Catholicism**, made to God; there are traditionally three: poverty, chastity and obedience

Vulgate the Latin version of the **scriptures**, as – very largely – translated by St Jerome towards the end of the fourth century

BIBLIOGRAPHY

The number of books on Catholicism in its many manifestations is immense. Those listed here are those which, for the most part, are reasonably accessible and a good starting point for further study. Included are the details of all the books referred to in the 'Further reading' sections at the end of each chapter, as well as those of a number of other works which may be of use, at least for purposes of consultation.

Annuarium Statisticum Ecclesiae (Vatican City: Libreria Editrice Vaticana, annual). A very detailed, annual survey published in several languages, in parallel columns, including Latin and English. Counts membership, Church personnel, Catholic institutions, number of baptisms, confirmations and a vast array of other statistics.

Assmann, Hugo, *Practical Theology of Liberation* (London: Search Press, 1975). Assmann was one of the senior figures in the Liberation Theology movement, at times rather difficult to understand. This, however, is a fairly simple introduction.

Barrett, David, Kurian, George and Johnson, Todd (eds), *World Christian Encyclopedia* (Oxford: Oxford University Press, 2001).

Fearsomely difficult to use, but has detailed statistics for every country and almost every Christian denomination.

Cardinale, Hyginus, *The Holy See and the International Order* (Gerrards Cross: Colin Smythe, 1976). A very detailed study of the mechanics of papal diplomacy. However, it is recommended here for the section on the legal status of the Holy See.

Catechism of the Catholic Church (2nd edition, London: Geoffrey Chapman, 1999). The *Catechism* was very controversial when it first appeared, and although it is a (semi-)official publication it bears evidence of the various hands, and schools of thought, which contributed to its compilation.

Coriden, James A., *An Introduction to Canon Law* (London: Burns and Oates, 2004).

Coriden, James A., *The Parish in Catholic Tradition* (New York: Paulist Press, 1996). A short, generally accessible study of the parish, including both the history of the institution and the canon law governing it.

Day, Peter, *Dictionary of Religious Orders* (London: Burns and Oates, 2001). Not a very good book, but there is nothing similar.

Duffy, Eamon, *Saints and Sinners* (London: Yale University Press, 1997). A one-volume, well-illustrated history of the papacy by an expert historian and elegant writer.

Dulles, Avery, *Models of the Church* (Dublin: Gill and Macmillan, 1988). A classic text on Catholic theories of the Church.

Fahlbusch, Erwin, Bromiley, Geoffrey W., Barrett, David B., Lochman, Jon M., Mbiti, John, Pelikan, Jaroslav and Vischer, Lukas (eds), *The Encyclopedia of Christianity* (Grand Rapids MI and Cambridge: Wm B. Eerdmans; Leiden: E. J. Brill, 1999–). Has excellent detailed entries (by David Barrett) on the religious situation/statistics of each country.

Farmer, David, *Oxford Dictionary of Saints* (5th edition, Oxford: Oxford University Press, 2003). Recommended for its excellent short discussion of saints and their place in Catholicism, but also one of the best general dictionaries of saints, though very far from inclusive.

Gutiérrez, Gustavo, *A Theology f Liberation* (London: SCM Press, 1974). The fundamental book on this subject, but not easy.

Hebblethwaite, Margaret, *Basic is Beautiful* (London: HarperCollins, 1993). A guidebook to the establishment of basic communities in the First World, but contains studies of them in Latin America, where the author has made her home.

Hill, Edmund, *Ministry and Authority in the Catholic Church* (London: Geoffrey Chapman, 1988), An excellent, well-laid-out survey of the role of authority in Catholicism, simple to use.

Kelly, J. N. D., *Early Christian Creeds* (3rd edition, London: Longman, 1972). A difficult but important book.

Kelly, J. N. D., *Oxford Dictionary of Popes* (Oxford: Oxford University Press, 1986). A standard work on papal history.

Lakeland, Paul, *The Liberation of the Laity* (New York: Continuum, 2000). A new theology of the laity, the tone of which may be gauged from the subtitle: 'A search for an accountable Church'.

McBrien, Richard, *Catholicism* (3rd edition, London: Geoffrey Chapman, 1994). A very popular, though rather massive, summary of Catholic belief. It is the third edition which is used in this text.

McBrien, Richard, *Encyclopedia of Catholicism* (San Francisco: HarperCollins, 1995). A bulky volume, but full of Catholic facts concisely recounted.

Nichols, Terence L., *That They May Be One* (Collegeville MN: Liturgical Press, 1997). An historical study of the role of hierarchy in the Catholic Church, including quite technical discussions of Vatican Councils I and II.

O'Collins, Gerald and Farrugia, Mario, *Catholicism: The Story of Catholic Christianity* (Oxford: Oxford University Press, 2003). An attractive, illustrated book which explains Catholicism, especially in relation to its historical context. Good on music, art and architecture.

O'Donnell, Christopher, *Ecclesia: A Thelogical Encyclopedia of the Church* (Collegeville MN: Liturgical Press, 1996). An excellent guide to the theology which underlies many of the topics covered in this book.

Osborne, Kenan, *Ministry: Lay Ministry in the Catholic Church* (Mahwah: Paulist Press, 1993). A very popular study.

Pollard, John F., *Money and the Rise of the Modern Papacy* (Cambridge: Cambridge University Press, 2004). Though it ends in 1950, the book explains the development of the Vatican's financial institutions

Quinn, John R., *The Reform of the Papacy* (New York: Crossroad, 1999). A series of lectures delivered in Oxford which has aroused much controversy within Catholicism. Quinn is an archbishop, and well acquainted with the topics he is discussing.

Rademacher, William J., *Lay Ministry* (New York: Crossroad, 1999). This is a book with a broad sweep, from the Bible to the present day. The edition quoted is a new study edition.

Reese, Thomas J., *Inside the Vatican* (Cambridge MA: Harvard University Press, 1996). Simply the best guide to the structures of the Vatican bureaucracy, and of the people who serve in it.

Rowland, Christopher, *Radical Christianity* (Cambridge: Polity Press, 1988). A study of various forms of radical Christianity, with a penultimate chapter on Liberation Theology.

Smart, Ninian (ed.), *Atlas of the World's Religions* (Oxford: Oxford University Press, 1999). There is a section on Christianity and pages showing the present spread of Christianity, including Catholicism.

Tanner, Norman P., *The Councils of the Church: A Short History* (New York: Crossroad Publishing, 2001). An excellent and very short guide to both the notion of councils, and their place in the history of Catholicism.

Tanner, Norman P. (ed.), *The Decrees of the Ecumenical Councils* (London: Sheed and Ward; Washington DC: Georgetown University Press, 1990). Two large volumes, the orginal language on one page, an English translation on the facing page. Important, but only for the dedicated.

Walsh, Michael, *The Conclave: A Sometimes Secret and Occasionally Bloody History of Papal Elections* (London: Canterbury Press; Chicago: Sheed and Ward, 2003). The history of the conclave, with a final chapter on how the modern conclave operates. It might also serve as a potted history of the papacy.

Walsh, Michael, *A Dictionary of Devotions* (Tunbridge Wells: Burns and Oates, 1993). A guide to the devotional practices of Catholics, feast days, shrines and so on.

Woodward, Kenneth L., *Making Saints* (London: Chatto and Windus, 1991). By far the best book on the processes within the Vatican about the creation of new saints. Good historical material too.

Young, Frances M., *The Making of the Creeds* (London: SCM Press; Philadelphia: Trinity Press, 1991). A much simpler, and shorter, introduction to the creeds than that by Kelly.

INDEX

Bold type indicates an entry in the glossary